THE KIDS THAT
ECOT TAUGHT

THE KIDS THAT ECOT TAUGHT

The Pioneers of America's
K–12 E-Schooling Revolution

BILL LAGER

EOS

PUBLISHING

PUBLISHING

For information, address EOS Publishing:
155 West Main Street, Suite 1206 Columbus, Ohio 43215
For information specifically regarding ECOT: www.ecotohio.org,
or write 3700 South High Street, Suite 95, Columbus, Ohio 43207.
info@ecotoh.org, or call 888-326-8395

Library of Congress Control Number: 2002093884

ISBN: 0-9723468-0-5

Printed in the United States of America

Managing Project Director: Robert Klaffky
Production Manager: Ruth Milligan
Managing Editor: Edith Delphia
Development Editor: Joan Paterson
Cover Designer and Print Coordinator: Spork Design
Printer: Typographic Printing Co.
Book Designer: Lisa Allen
Indexer: Rachel Rice

To Tom Baker, Superintendent of Lucas County
Educational Service Center

Pioneers are the ones who make things happen.
Thank you, Tom, for being our pioneer.
We wouldn't be here without you.

and to

Joshua Baird, an ECOT student

Joshua will always be the most inspirational person
I have ever had the pleasure of knowing.
He uniquely represents all of the thousands of students
and parents who braved the difficult first year of ECOT.
Young people like Joshua remind us every day why the sun rises.

CONTENTS

CONTENTS

CONTENTS

CONTENTS

INTRODUCTION

The graduates of the Electronic Classroom of Tomorrow Class of 2001 are pioneers of education. Their 21 diplomas will be collector's items some day. While they sat concentrating at their computers, they had no idea they were making history, but they were. These students were the first graduating class from a K–12 online school in the country. As the kids might say, "This is tight!"

I want you to meet these daring youngsters and share their excitement for life. I want you to know what was going on behind the scenes as this revolution in education was unfolding before our eyes. It wasn't always pretty—most business start-ups aren't. The determination of these 21 remarkable young adults was a major factor in helping us focus on overcoming the not-so-pretty parts. All of us involved in the first year of the Electronic Classroom of Tomorrow (ECOT) held their hopes and dreams in our hearts as we forged ahead, convinced that our efforts would make a difference to so many children.

As consumers, we have gotten used to perfection in our culture, expecting it immediately from any enterprise we do business with. As you read through the chapters, you will see that ECOT could not initially meet that standard, for a variety of reasons. As electronic schools form around the country, however, I hope that they will be inspired by ECOT's story and encouraged by ECOT's success. I know that our mistakes and sleepless nights as my colleagues and I developed ECOT will help other e-schools to form without as much anguish. We fought battles and solved problems that no one will have to solve again.

Would we do it again? In a mouse click! So many people have put their souls and sweat into making the first K–12 electronic school in Ohio happen. They all have the satisfaction of knowing that they have been part of the beginning of something. What that something will become is yet to be discovered. I have my own predictions, but you and every other person in this country who cares about kids will be part of the decision-making team that will help the local school boards, state legislatures, and lawmakers in Washington make choices in education.

Starting a K–12 e-school was like staring at a mountain. Why climb it? Because it's there. The only difference? Every day the mountain grew and we had to climb it again. No one had been to the top before. No one had drawn any maps, left any blazes, or cleared any trails. In fact, folks had left land mines, booby traps, and false signal fires, convinced that the top was just too scary for anyone to reach.

People have used a variety of adjectives to describe me, but timid doesn't usually make the list. Make a challenge more difficult and I work harder to stay in the game. It's a tough lesson for my detractors to learn; every time they looked for ways to derail this amazing discovery, they made me stronger. If they had just let me figure out for myself how ridiculously difficult it would be to make this work, I probably would have failed and not be around today to cause them headaches. It was their insistence that I couldn't or shouldn't start this school that made me more determined.

I sometimes wonder where that determination came from. And more importantly, how it found its way to help me stay standing throughout the incessant blows thrown my way in the last two years. Why did a guy from a neighborhood in west Columbus called The Bottoms (it was as bad as it sounds), who made and lost his first fortune in the office equipment business, decide to start the first K–12 e-school in Ohio? Like many passions, this one caught me off guard. I was well into the project, getting up each morning to attack a new windmill, before I really understood it myself.

It has to do with two women whom ECOT did not teach. They are two women whom I love deeply—two of the most brilliant women I have ever known. They taught me more than all my years of schooling combined, in spite of the fact that the public school settings available to them failed them after sixth grade.

Mildred was my mother, my soulmate, and my teacher. As a young girl in Lawrence County, Ohio, her schooling ended in sixth grade because the economic realities of the depression forced her to enter the workforce. She spent her teen years working in a shoe factory in Portsmouth. Her love of books was a guiding force in my life and I still read four or five books a week. She sacrificed any luxury in her life to be able to send my four siblings and me to Catholic schools. We had nothing but education and, therefore, we had everything that mattered.

Bethany is my stepdaughter, a child I was blessed to have come into my life when I married her mother. Her juvenile diabetes was a struggle for her, as it is for any child. The schools were ill equipped to help her keep up with her schoolwork. There were months when she spent more time in Children's Hospital than in school. Being sick is hard enough; falling behind at school takes a terrible toll on a youngster who understandably needs to feel normal and fit in with her friends. I fought for her right to be educated and found solutions in expensive private schools that I was fortunate enough to be able to afford.

As I fought to support Bethany a dozen years ago, I wondered what my friends back in the old neighborhood would do when faced with the same realities. Today, I know that they can send their children to ECOT. There is no word for how proud it makes me feel.

ECOT has become a solution for the most diverse group of students anyone could imagine. As you meet the Class of '01, I hope you will see how special each and every child is to me and to our society. We can't afford to abandon any child, especially when we have the ability to educate children at any place, on any path, at any pace.

GRADUATES OF
THE ECOT CLASS OF 2001

Candice Adams

Jaclyn Cartier

Chondra Cline

Lisa Darrow

Autumn Davis

Angela Feliciano

James Gerity

Ryan Heilig

Jacob Keach

Karita McDermitt

Wendy Napier

Elizabeth Neal

Jennifer Perkins

Shannon Pounds

Jessica Ricciardo

Mandi Riebel

Theresa Roth

Stefanie Taylor

Vera Vest

Quiana Watson

Richard Wolff

ACKNOWLEDGEMENTS

This book is a culmination of two years of the most difficult, but truly rewarding, work of my and many others' lives.

Before acknowledging those who assisted me in compiling this book, it is necessary that I bring deserved and needed recognition to those individuals who have helped build ECOT into the largest charter school in the country. Without the dedication of our board, staff, teachers, consultants, and friends, we would still be an idea on a napkin.

But let me start with the group of individuals who matter most—our students and their parents. I could take pages of this book to describe how grateful I am, and the whole staff is, for the commitment and involvement of every single student and parent. We would not be a school today if it weren't for them.

The Board of the Lucas County Educational Service Center who authorized the charter for ECOT and have weathered more storms than your local meteorologist: Karen Krause, president; Joe Rutherford, vice-president; Randy Dixon, member; Judy Hansen, member; Joan Kuchcinski, member; and Tom Baker, superintendent. The employees of the Lucas County Educational Service Center are also to be singled out for their untiring efforts on behalf of ECOT and all the schools they sponsor.

ECOT Board members who have guided us through the toughest of storms include Sherri Dembinski, chairman; Cindy Baird, member; Donald F. Wihl, member; and Donna Wihl, board secretary.

A very honored thanks to State Representative Jon Peterson,

ECOT's first commencement speaker, and to David Varda for his efforts on behalf of ECOT and the Ohio Department of Education.

Jeffrey P. Forster, superintendent of ECOT, leads an amazingly dedicated team of teaching professionals who devote countless energy and time to each of our high school students: Martha Bycynski, director of education and ECOT's first Employee of the Year, James Lampert, high school principal, Beverly Beutell, Keith Birkhold, Jennifer Boyer, Todd Cook, Eric Davis, Soren Fanning, Janet Fisher, Nancy Grandillo, Marilyn Hiestand, Deborah Lampert, Marian Maxfield, Tadd Maxfield, Mark Palen, Lawana Partlow, Deborah Poynor, Steven Reeves, Linda Roberts, Duncan Schaefer, Michael Schmidt, Jeannine Staller, Jennifer Theiss, Robert Townsend, Dawn Varner, Leigha Wells, and Patricia Younce.

ECOT's Middle School, led by its dedicated Principal Ted Tway: John Bereza, Laura Bowling, Jay Bowman, Maria Boyarko, Caroline Buoni, Ruth Cline, Janet Depinet, Jennifer Erickson, Alexis Finley, Melissa Finley, Diane King, Mary Jo Lorenzi, Michelle Rorabaugh, Mary Smiley, Susan Smith, and Patricia Whetsel.

ECOT's Elementary School, directed by its Principal Patrick Barrett: Maria Biondo, Sarah Castle, Cathy Craiglow, Melanie Davis, Renee DeLuca, Jill Dolan, Ellen French, Brenda Gibson, Sandy Haskins, Vicki Hopkins, James Jones, Sandy Kelly, Ellen Lepage, Rosemary Mullen, Katie Setty, Daren Thomas, Jennifer Thomas, Anna Trachsel, Beth Wadlington, Darlene Welling, and Mollie Wertz.

ECOT's Exceptional Children group, managed by Linda Lowry-Logsdon: Mandy Baker, Margaret Blake, Carol Byers, Karole K. Byers, Maria Cannon, Pat Evans, Kathryn Haeger, Kristin Harris, Beaulah Hartge, Melissa Julian, Mary Latimer, Mary Massey, Talea McGuinnis, Tracy Novotny, Lori Patricia Saum, Diana Scoff, Jill Shamis, and Nicole Wilson.

ECOT's outstanding educational support staff consists of Vernell Bristow, Earl Burnett, Patricia Felts, and Karen Smith.

Scott W. Kern, chief of operations, who heads up an extremely devoted administrative staff: Jan Attanasio, Marlo Berry, Teresa Berry, James Calabrese, Lanetta Cannon, Katy Corban, Manda Craft, Rose Faber, Kimberly Fender, Connie Jacobs, Ryan Johnson, Pat Kosmoski, Carol Krecsmar, Steve Ledingham, Jerry Margeson, Jeremy Pennington, Becki Shallenberger, Gwen Simmons, Chandra Wilcox, Nick Wilson, and Kellee Workman.

Steve Ramsey, executive director of the Ohio Charter School Association and his board of Tom Baker, chairman; Richard Lukich, member; James Cowardin, member; Susan Ducks, member; and Ann Higdon, member; are to be commended for their unwavering leadership in the charter school movement, as are Clint Satow and Anita Nelam from the Ohio Community School Center.

A host of corporate partners including Xerox Corporation: John T. Mirosovich, Kevin Pichardt, Bob Hope; Xerox Connect: David Frazekas, Jeff Blain, Ed Driscoll, Jeff Drew, Chris Collins; Compaq Corporation: Mark Dennis, Steve Handy; Information Leasing Corporation: Vince Rinaldi, Jeff Weiner; Learn.com: Patrick Toomey; Compass Learning Odyssey (formerly ChildU): Trisha Foster; King Copy: Jack King; Intertel: Jeff Blair; Ameritech: John McKenna, Lee Connors; Voyager.net/CoreComm: Dave Schroeder; Benefits Network Associates: Jim Guessford; Berwanger Overmeyer: Chuck Merlin; Brothers Office Supply: Kurt Schmeltzer, Murray Schmeltzer; Signs USA: Chuck Riley; Bob Evans Corporation: Judy Long; Barbara DeSalvo; Business MAP Ltd.: Jo Neal; Olde Fashioned Services: Bill Flynn; Bradley Equipment Company: Don Bradley.

A number of consultants worked with me tirelessly to assure that all systems were in place so that ECOT could serve its 3,000 students. Their loyalty to the project was unprecedented. They include George Anderson with Uvonics Co. Inc.; Amy J. Borman, attorney-at-law with Eastman & Smith Ltd.; Michael Bradley with Bradley & Associates; Glenn Fickle with Glenn Allen Associates; Robert F.

Klaffky with Van Meter, Ashbrook & Associates; Zita Hunt, CPA with Whalen & Co., CPAs; Melanie Looney with the Center for Education Reform, Washington, DC; James Maniace, Esq., with Swedlow, Butler, Levine, Lewis & Dye Co. L.P.A.; Brian T. Usher with Capital Communications Alliance; Ed Hogan with New Visions Group; Bill Hines, superintendent of the Vilas School District, Vilas, Colorado.

Before I even knew what a charter school was, a number of truly visionary public policy makers within Ohio paved uncharted territory to allow for the charter school movement to begin. In the beginning, former state of Ohio Representatives Michael A. Fox and Sally Perz had the idea. It truly started with them. Former State Rep. Pat Tiberi (now U.S. Congressman), championed parental choice, while State Rep. Jon Husted showed incredible intestinal fortitude as a freshman legislator to fight for important legislation for charter school laws against the power of the education establishment. State Auditor Jim Petro offered incredible oversight in making the Ohio Department of Education do its job; he was the needed check and balance to assure proper management of all charter schools. Many members of the Ohio House and Senate spent long hours and careful thought in deliberating over controversial issues that ultimately moved the ball forward. And finally, last but certainly not least, thanks to Speaker of the House of Representatives Larry Householder, for without his leadership and foresight this movement would be lost.

Several key business leaders such as the late Don Ettore, Dave Brennan, and Checker Finn responded to the public policy changes regarding charter schools and, likely, influenced their development well before I decided to start ECOT. While we may be competitors, they deserve recognition, nonetheless, for their perseverance that allowed individuals like me to embrace and pursue the dream of providing alternative and effective channels of education for the youth of Ohio.

My personal friends who have stuck with me during many years of personal challenges, not just the thousands we overcame with ECOT, include Martha Linkous, Jack and Sue McKenna, Dean Rogers, Mark Sebastian, Roy Orr, Pauline Wessa, Sandra Barklow, Teresa Berry, Brad and Kathy Martensen, Pat and Rhonda Cahill, JR Dembinski, Judy Dobbins, Ryan Weddle, Howard Mitchell, David Dobos, Dr. John A. Leddingham Jr., Nina Green, Dale Moore, Jerry Meyer, Robert Pfefferle, Richard Ferguson, CPA, Steve Wilson, Kathleen Nash, Jim Ankowski, Betty Moon, David O. Niehoff, Stephen J. Smith, and especially Susan Richardson, my personal aide, confidant, and friend.

Now, about this book. Bob Klaffky gets the credit (or blame?) for introducing me to the Milligan sisters, Edie and Ruth, who have guided every step of this publication process. Thanks to them for their patience with me and to their talented team including Susan Richardson, Joan Paterson, Drew Robinson, Dominic LaRiccia, Lisa Allen, Rachel Rice, and Heather Brown, who have helped me successfully capture the spirit and essence of ECOT through the eyes of our first graduating class. May there be many more graduates to document in years to come.

FOREWORD

If anyone can survive the troubles that life brings without losing sight of who they are or what they stand for, it is my father. I have seen him endure a lot of difficulties, but he always manages to express kindness, shrewdness, humor, stubbornness, competitiveness, and love.

My father told me something that has always stayed with me, "You're only a failure, if you fail to stand up to your defeats." There have been many times when he has fallen, but he has never failed. After he has been knocked down, in no time he is back, ready to continue to fight for what he believes in.

Watching him do this has given me the confidence to carry on whenever I encounter difficult situations in my own life. Whether it is a problem at school or with my friends or family, I have been able to follow my father's example. It is hard to try again for something that you did not succeed in attaining the first time. But people must go on or the world will become nothing more than a haven for those without goals or aspirations. Ideas would not develop; no one would flourish.

I learned many things from my father's work with ECOT. I learned that failures can be helpful hindrances on the path to success. Sure, I had heard that before, but I did not truly understand the meaning until I saw examples of obstructions in my father's life. Each obstacle made him stronger. And with each of ECOT's problems came a lesson that made ECOT more successful than before.

When you fail in something that is important to you and decide to continue on, only success can follow. Because of people like my father, children who would not normally be able to attend school can through ECOT. Instead of being left behind, these children are able to experience the greatest gift of all: knowledge.

The Electronic Classroom of Tomorrow had its share of good and bad times during the first two years of its existence. Sometimes it seemed as if the negative incidents stretched their shadow in an attempt to suffocate the positive goals that ECOT was trying to accomplish: critics reported harmful viewpoints; public schools protested its existence; teacher unions waged war against it. My father confronted so many obstacles during ECOT's development it is a wonder he did not give up. However, he is not the type to abandon something in which he believes, no matter how hard the struggle. The trials and tribulations hit my father hard but he stuck with ECOT—standing tall, confident, and never wavering.

When you fail in something important to you and decide to continue on, only success can follow. I know because I have witnessed this in my father's life. I have learned that success does not make the person—the person makes the success. Prosperity that you may experience is temporary; it can fade away at any moment. The principles and values of a person last forever—that is where real worth lies. As you read this book, you will come to understand how a person's beliefs and ideas continue on in the face of adversity, just as I learned from my father.

JESSICA LAGER

1

e IS FOR EXPANSION

"Frederick Douglass once said that '[e]ducation ... means emancipation. It means light and liberty. It means the uplifting of the soul of man into the glorious light of truth, the light by which men can only be made free.' Today many of our inner-city public schools deny emancipation to urban minority students. Despite this Court's observation nearly 50 years ago in *Brown v. Board of Education*, that 'it is doubtful that any child may reasonably be expected to succeed in life if he is denied the opportunity of an education,'... urban children have been forced into a system that continually fails them."

**United States Supreme Court Justice
Clarence Thomas
Concurring Opinion in
Zelman v. Simmons-Harris, June, 2002**

The availability of accredited public education delivered electronically into a student's home is a natural and needed expansion of the public education movement that started over 150 years ago. Notice I said expansion, not replacement. So many black-and-white thinkers look at a new idea and immediately see an either/or proposition: Either we try this new concept or we get to keep what we know as normal. By expanding the role of computers in the delivery of education, we will achieve levels of efficiency and effectiveness never before imagined.

The generation graduating from high school today saw the evolution of personal computers and the Internet into their lives. The next generation will see the integration of electronic education into every child's life as an expansion of traditional public education, not as a replacement. Electronic education is here; it's now; and it's not going away. The exciting question ahead of us is how to use it for the betterment of education, children, and society as a whole.

Electronic education models hold the promise to accomplish everything from reducing the dropout rate to addressing the school funding crisis[1] to easing the impact of teacher shortages to providing special-needs students with access to the education they need. Electronic education will be the vehicle for eliminating the digital divide, the cultural and economic inequity that exists between those with computer access and literacy and those without. Electronic education models also allow more choice in curriculum at less cost, flexibility in scheduling, increased parent involvement, and a self-paced learning environment.

Even with all that promise, you would expect the beginning of anything this revolutionary to be rocky. Our impatient world rarely allows systems to be in place and fully tested before they are available. People are understandably skeptical of innovation, often critical, and sometimes hostile. Regulatory agencies aren't built to respond to change positively. The media thrive on the negative and the failures. Critics with "I-told-you-so" attitudes will use each new piece of negative information to dig their heels in further. Throughout the following chapters I will describe the rocks we hit on our road to creating this new approach to education. We have pushed many of these rocks out of the way, making the path easier for those who follow. Many obstacles still exist, however, and will only be cleared as the stakeholders in this discussion begin to see the revolutionary opportunities that exist for our children.

The kids that ECOT taught are now young adults who came to Ohio's first statewide K–12 e-school as seniors in high school and received their diplomas in June 2001 as the first graduating class of this pioneering school. They have shared their stories of growing up in a variety of educational settings before completing their high school education at the Electronic Classroom of Tomorrow (ECOT), the charter school that I founded. Their collective voice shouts from the rooftops of the tremendous positive power that an e-school can have for a child.

Their stories speak of the unmatched courage it takes to be the first at something. As literally hundreds of news stories were hitting the wires about our problems during their senior year, the students were online doing their homework. As the Ohio Department of Education was changing our guidelines almost weekly, the students were online studying for tests. As our staff was working long hours every weekend to make sure the school got off the ground, the students were online e-mailing their teachers. They just kept going, signing online and learning. Some left due to the pressures, challenges, and obstacles of our start-up year, but our graduates kept going. They knew their diploma was something worth striving for. What they didn't know was how important their determination was in the fight to open up the world of e-learning to children everywhere.

At the beginning of each chapter, you will meet one of these accidental pioneers. Each student came to ECOT for a different reason. Some because they were bored, some because they were ignored. Some were looking for safety in an increasingly dangerous world and some were looking to provide security for family members by staying home with them. Some were looking for flexibility to work a full-time job or flexibility to work at their own pace with their schoolwork. Some were focused on where they were going and how ECOT could get them there faster; some were lost in a public education system that didn't have a roadmap for them.

Entrepreneurs search their entire lives for a waiting market—a demand that has not yet been serviced by existing producers of goods and services. What were these students demanding that traditional public schools weren't providing? What resources were available that could meet their need? Bringing these resources to this market was a challenge that captured my entire attention the moment it occurred to me. You will learn that our initial announcement of the school was not purposeful, but instead leaked to the media. As our voicemail box filled up with 400 calls every hour, we knew we had a waiting market. And these were just what marketers call the "early adopters." Imagine how many people would become interested as the early adopters spread the word!

Several years ago *Inc. Magazine* surveyed their Inc. 500 list of top entrepreneurs in the country. One question stood out in my mind: How many companies did you start before this one (that made it to the Inc. 500)? The startling average was seven! Seven times tried and failed. Seven times thinking they had stumbled on a great idea and then watched it wither away. Seven times having to send their employees home, never to return. Seven times having to deal with creditors. Yet they did it just one more time and became heroes of industry.

Two questions arise out of this collective experience: Why did they do it again and again and was it acquired insight or luck that made the last attempt successful?

Entrepreneurs have been studied and analyzed to the point of exhaustion. Yet it isn't totally understood why we find our passion in untested, unproven, risky enterprises that often end in disaster. And then, we pick ourselves up and do it again. For me, it is the chase, the climb, the challenge. What are we looking for in that uncharted territory? The waiting market—an unmet demand—a new way to bring together capital and labor to create a product consumers want.

So we come back again, each time with the bitter taste of failure in our mouths. But there we are: living, breathing, thinking, creating. The failure didn't kill us but instead taught us our strengths and limits. We know where to push next time. And we know the warning signs to watch for. We learn more from our failures than from our successes. Entrepreneurs have more tolerance for failure than most people. Each time we take a new risk, we calculate it a little more exactly.

Contrary to popular belief, entrepreneurs are not motivated by money or profits. Businessmen and women are motivated by money—solving the puzzle motivates entrepreneurs. The bottom line merely tells us whether we did it or not. We know how to use money and profits to further refine the solution. We don't like solving puzzles other people have already put together. If there is an answer key somewhere, we're immediately bored. We like the discovery and the thrill of seeing the treasure before anyone else does.

Once we find a hidden market, entrepreneurs like to hide it from others for a short time until we figure out our business strategy. Timing is critical. If we wait too long, someone else is bound to figure it out or consumers will move on to other needs (in the case of fads.) If we act too quickly, we run the risk of going to market too soon and providing less than a quality product. In the case of ECOT, our timing was determined by the guidelines for charter schools. We were given five months from the day that our charter was approved to the first day of school. I'm pretty sure I couldn't plan a wedding in that period of time (and given my track record with marriages, probably shouldn't!).

Waiting another school year was not an option, so we had to do what we could, the best we could. For many, it wasn't good enough and still isn't. For 3,000 students and their parents, it's a miracle. They had been waiting for a solution to the problem of how to educate their children that would work for them. Somehow, the other choices available to them were not optimal. ECOT met their needs. These parents are our inspiration as we continue to travel along this rocky road. As consumers, parents are purchasing the most precious commodity they will ever choose: their children's futures. It is not an accident that we are currently the largest school in Ohio and the largest charter school in the country. In the marketplace, where willing buyers and willing sellers get together to meet the needs of children, the buyers and sellers were not consummating their transactions in the traditional sense of exchanging money for service. Instead, the buyers were making market decisions by abandoning one system in exchange for another.

An interesting television advertisement recently ran for United Parcel Service. It showed the employees of an Internet start-up company standing around a computer screen as the company launches its Web site. The room is tense as the hit counter begins to turn. Cheers ring out! They're in business! Then anxiety takes over as their success brings them to a point of saturation and beyond. How will they ever fill all those orders? The solution, we are told, is UPS.

Now you know what it was like as ECOT began. Nowhere in our wildest imaginations did we anticipate a demand close to what we experienced. Other online schools have not seen the same surge. Their steady growth, however, is evidence that electronic education is not a fad. We apparently solved the puzzle. In the chapters that follow, I will outline the solution as I now know it. Each day brings new and exciting changes that continue to serve the market better.

These were the pieces that I started with, as the puzzle of fixing the problems with public education became my passion:

- Public education continues to be important to our society even as parents are demanding more choices for their children.

- Public school systems in some areas are limited in their ability to provide a safe and effective learning environment. Charter schools have been invited by state legislatures to provide alternatives.

- Certain types of students do not respond well to the traditional public school system as it is currently designed. These include academically gifted and learning disabled students, physically and mentally handicapped students, and older dropouts.

- Technological advances in the last five years allow for new and creative delivery systems for educational experiences.

- Parents provide a positive and cost-effective influence in the education process. Homeschooling is on the rise with parents taking primary roles in their children's education.

- Computer literacy will be a key component of vocational success for most students throughout their lives.

- Education will be a life-long activity, with much of adult learning and research resources delivered electronically.

Most people would agree that all the above statements are true. Some are so obvious as to be invisible to those who may be looking for solutions to the education crisis in the country. And who would know that the combination of these premises would lead to a conclusion that looked like ECOT? Initially, only myself and my close associates who signed on early to watch the solution hatch. And now, thousands of families who have consciously chosen ECOT to meet their unique needs. As much as it has solved the puzzle, ECOT represents only one of many possible models for electronic education.

The entire notion of charter schools is to bring innovative thinking to the problem of our failing public schools. People who work inside the existing system would naturally start with what they have and make adjustments to that system. They have pride of ownership in what has already been built and the prospect of tearing it down to build a brand-new system meets with insurmountable roadblocks in most organizations. Charter schools were created to be incubators for new ideas that would never make it out of committee in a large school district. However, the established public education system is powerful enough to make sure that the charter schools don't have an easy road. One by one, each charter school succeeds not because it's just a good idea, but a great idea. Each has a leader who is motivated by the quest for quality in a world of discouraging performance by many established public school systems.

The mandate from the lawmakers who invited entrepreneurs to develop charter schools in Ohio is vague. Be innovative, but not too much so. Be financially stable, but don't use accepted sources of capital that work well for other types of businesses. Follow the rules, but don't expect to know what they are until after the fact. Compete for students and funding from your local school district, but don't expect respect when you win that competition. Be a business, but don't act too much like one. Strive for excellence, but don't expect recognition if you find it. They could not have foreseen all the issues needing attention at the time and are working hard to eliminate some of the early confusion.

All of this probably makes you wonder why anyone would continue fighting this battle under these circumstances. It seems to be the only front open in the challenge to improve our failing school systems. Reformers have a difficult time first of all getting elected to school boards and then making any changes once elected. School funding is so confusing that it is hard to know when a "no" vote for a levy or bond issue is sending any message or ending up detrimental to the students. Letters to the editor can complain and letters to the school board can plead, but many things in the traditional education system continue to deteriorate. Dropout rates are the highest they have ever been in many districts, proficiency scores seem impossible to budge, and good teachers are harder to retain.

The only decision left is for parents to send their children to school elsewhere. Choice is now a watchword for the reality that parents are tired of putting up with the status quo of below-par educational options. As charter schools and other school choice programs[2] find cracks in the door to sneak through, real change may occur.

Change is threatening to the established public school industry, which includes the teachers' unions, the superintendents, the school boards, the PTAs, and the state departments. Think about it, though. What other industry has their research done for them for free? Each new charter school is an incubator for studying new concepts and approaches to education. Instead of hiding behind new ways to measure old failures, the public school industry could embrace the volunteer work by the tireless entrepreneurs who are developing charter schools. Their results could be incorporated into their systems fully documented.

One option for school districts is to concentrate on their strengths and let charter schools pick up areas that aren't economical to provide. The e-schooling option, especially, has the power to let districts subcontract to specialists who might service multiple districts. Universities have been offering distance learning for a long time—the product has been tested and proven, just not at the K–12 level. It takes a new mindset to envision what this will look like for K–12 learning. More than that, however, e-schooling will require a new system of paying for education. Entrepreneurs will only be attracted to the market if the market shows its willingness to pay for their products.

This is a complicated puzzle to solve, even though the premises are fairly simple. In the chapters that follow, I will lay out the story of how this solution evolved and how it has already changed through the discovery of mistaken assumptions and unforeseen obstacles. As other e-schools begin across the country, it is my sincere hope that our experience will serve as a beacon for what, and more importantly, what not, to do in order to be successful.

Then we will explore together the horizon for where this concept can take us. It is exciting to some people and scary to others. The stakes are too high not to try. The market has already sent a strong signal in the form of ECOT's immediate, very high enrollment. The opposition we have encountered is additional proof that we might be on to something.

NOTES

1. Ohio has been under an Ohio Supreme Court order for several years to revise the school funding formulas to reduce the discrepancy between the rich and poor districts in the state. The Court is still considering the solutions proposed by the legislature.

2. Ohio made national headlines with the U.S. Supreme Court decision overturning a challenge to a school voucher program that has been tested in the Cleveland Public School District.

Graduate Profile:

CANDICE

When Candice learned that my mother had not had the opportunity to get a high school education, something suddenly made sense to her. The entire time she was working toward her high school diploma, she had wondered, "Why are they doing this for me? It doesn't make any sense. It's too good to be true."

As a new wife and mother living on a newlywed's income, Candice could not afford the cost of daycare to allow her to return to high school. And she did not want to miss out on breastfeeding her son. However, she couldn't see herself raising a child without setting the example of completing a high school education.

Candice married at 16, in December of her junior year. Her husband, five years her senior, refused to marry her unless she promised to stay in school and get her diploma. He had made the mistake of dropping out during his senior year to get a job. Later, although he did receive his Graduate Equivalency Diploma (G.E.D.), he regretted his decision and didn't want Candice to follow his example.

Candice had transferred that year to the Eastland Career Center, southeast of Columbus, from the Canal Winchester schools that she had attended since Kindergarten. She transferred to study cosmetology, a career she anticipated would support her while she studied to become a massage therapist. Within days after the wedding, however, she contracted mononucleosis, causing her to miss several weeks of school. Just as she returned to school, she learned she was pregnant. This baby was unplanned, though never unloved.

As a married pregnant student at the Career Center, Candice watched the attitudes of her classmates toward her change. This social pressure on top of her physical challenges, her missed schoolwork when she was sick, and the financial reality of the new baby caused her to drop out. She then found a desk job that lasted for a couple of months until complications from the pregnancy sent her home to wait for the birth of her son.

Candice was disappointed that it didn't look as if she would be able to finish high school. Resigned to the fact that she would have to break her promise to her husband and get a G.E.D., she shared her feelings with her parents. Her Dad had heard about the opening of ECOT on the radio and told her to check it out. Candice was skeptical, thinking it would cost money, which she didn't have. When she called, however, it was like a dream come true.

Candice received her computer about a month after she enrolled, went to work immediately, and set herself a goal of making up the eleventh-grade credits she had missed and graduating on time. Our counselors initially had difficulty getting her into the right courses, which set her back a few weeks, but she still completed all her courses by June.

During these months, her husband was working very long hours—sometimes away overnight—and was usually sleeping when he was home. Candice cared for her son around the clock, working on her schoolwork whenever he slept and often holding him while she worked.

Some nights she worked until 3 a.m. She and the baby were on their own schedule.

Candice felt that the coursework at ECOT was more rigorous than her classes in the Canal Winchester schools. She attributed this to the fact that the teachers weren't right there to look over her shoulder to keep her working. She accepted ECOT's requirements, however. It never occurred to her to complain. This was a chance at earning a diploma she never expected to have. And there was her beautiful child that she was able to care for—it was more than she could ask for.

After Candice graduated, she signed up for a home study e-course in medical transcribing. She has completed this course and is working for an area doctor from her home. She feels her comfort on the computer was greatly enhanced by her computer hours at ECOT. She never felt frustrated with the new computer skills she was learning and uses them each day in her career.

Her role as a mother has changed her perspective about education. She fears the direction that schools are headed in and worries about her son's safety in the future. She saw firsthand the increase in drug use and wonders how a mother can protect her son from such dangers, when her experience was that most schools turn and look the other way. She'd love to have him grow up in a good school system with friends and activities he enjoys. She wonders if that is a dream that won't come true.

2

KEEPING THE GAME ALIVE

"If it were not for ECOT, my child would be looking
at two parents without high school diplomas.
That is not acceptable."

Candice Adams, ECOT Class of '01

For the last three years, my entire world has been devoted to two things: raising my teenage daughter and starting ECOT. Both are precious to me and both give me so much in return. You met Jessica in the Foreword that she wrote. Her education choices have been positive and I am a proud father, happy to see that she will be attending Wittenberg University in the fall of 2002. Jessica attended both public and Catholic schools. She is a wonderful learner and would love to write for a career some day. She has watched this book unfold with interest and excitement. As any father knows, all the business accomplishments in the world don't compare to the love and respect of a child.

I guess that now is the moment that I have to admit that I am not 24 years old anymore and that I did have a life before ECOT and even before Jessica. The mystery of how I arrived at the decision to build ECOT and found the solution to this education puzzle is drawn from my experiences throughout my life, which has been sprinkled with good days and bad days, just like anyone else's life. I feel blessed on the good days and try to learn from the bad days.

Columbus has been my home all my life. My father grew up on a farm in St. Joseph, Missouri. His family lost the farm during the depression and moved to Columbus about the time that he enlisted in World War II. My mother grew up on the Ohio River and found her way to Columbus, looking for work. They met at the old Curtis Wright plant, later taken over by Rockwell. They had five children including two sets of twins a year apart. As one of the younger twins, I grew up with three very close siblings and one brother, many years older. I grew up in a neighborhood that was the first historical settlement in the area, called Franklinton. It evolved to be referred to as The Bottoms, partially because it was in a flood plane and partially because the name fit.

If you were to go back to that time and ask, "Where was Columbus's ghetto?" you would probably pick the street I lived on.

The houses were built in the 1880s, clapboard, with two bedrooms. I don't want to sound like Abraham Lincoln but it was a poor neighborhood. One thing I remember more than anything else is that my parents, although they were not educated, put education above every other value. The fact that they managed to send their kids through Catholic school and pay tuition and all the other expenses related to a private school when they didn't have much money is testimony to the fact that they put education first. They were actively involved in the school. If you look at where I grew up, school was all there was. School became the focus of our family because it was the only way out of The Bottoms.

While Catholic schools, in my opinion, don't necessarily deliver the best education or have the best resources to deliver the best education, they gave us a sense of discipline and a respect for education. While my mother was not educated, she was a brilliant woman with a strong intuitive sense. She knew her kids and the world well and developed a sense of the world that was very insightful.

For a reason that I never discovered, my mother latched onto me as the one kid in the family who had a shot. As a result, I was the only one who went to college and bypassed the blue-collar lifestyle. When I was a young child, we would sit and talk as she got ready for work. We would watch the "Today Show" with Dave Garroway and talk about what was happening in the world. My ability to discover my world came from my mother's pointing the way. Early on I became aware of the world I lived in. Other than her misuse of certain language or the fact that she couldn't write, you would never know that my mother was anything but smart.

Her encouragement was focused and, at times, pretty rough on me. She was the one in my life who asked, "Why are you screwing around when you can do better? You have the ability. Why are you lazy?" She used motivational skills, positive and negative, to say, "Look, you've got it. You can do it. Don't waste your resources."

Although we were poor, it was her efforts, along with my father's, of course, that allowed us to go to Catholic school. They both believed that we would get a better education along with a better set of values, discipline, and respect at Catholic schools. So, we did without. We never went on a vacation until I was a senior in high school; there simply wasn't enough money.

There was always enough money for uniforms, however. I recall that when I became interested in art, there were always enough paints and brushes around. If I became interested in reading, there were enough books. When my brothers and I became interested in music and had a band in high school, there were musical instruments and music lessons. There was always plenty of opportunity for things that would help us learn. My parents held the philosophy that it was their job to give their kids an opportunity to jump to a higher level.

I attended Holy Family elementary school from K–8 and then went to Bishop Ready High School. While in high school, I was elected class president all four years, elected mayor of Columbus Youth in Government Day in a citywide school election, attended Buckeye Boy's State, where I was runner-up for governor. As I was an opinion leader in high school, I became a social leader and editor of the school newspaper.

After high school, I went to Ohio State University for three years with a 3.5 accumulated average. I left OSU during the Vietnam War to enlist in the U.S. Coast Guard Reserve. I was based on the cutter "Tanager," which patrolled the East Coast of the U.S. I became a veteran of the United States Coast Guard and never returned to college.

While still in college, I became active in local Democratic politics and was on the local civic council at Hilltop (the neighborhood next to The Bottoms). I was president of the Hilltop Community Council and a trustee of the Grandview Heights Civic Association. I was doing all the basic political drills, working as a volunteer and fundraiser on several campaigns for state representatives, state senators, and city council representatives. I was elected vice president of Young Democrats at age 19 and became president when the acting president resigned. I was a candidate to be a delegate to the 1972 National Democratic Convention.

While at Ohio State, I worked for two years for the Ohio Attorney General William J. Brown, and became his business manager after I returned from the Coast Guard. I was actively prepared and willing to seek office myself in the 1972–1973 period. This was the time when the vote was given to 18-year-olds and the political parties sought young people as candidates. Early on I gave scores of speeches to groups ranging from 20 to 100 people.

Just at the time I was prepared to run for office and the party officials were ready to see me throw my hat in the ring, there was a tragedy in my family. One of my older twin brothers had developed a mental illness, paranoid schizophrenia, exactly as depicted in the movie "A Beautiful Mind." I lived through that experience as one of his caregivers for a year.

As my political career was beginning to blossom, my brother murdered someone and then committed suicide. His name and, therefore, my name became a news story. At the time, the negative publicity was the least of my pain but soon the phones stopped ringing for a period of a year or two. Politics forgives many mistakes, but that was one I couldn't correct.

I reluctantly put my political ambitions aside and at age 23 started Office Works, an office supply, furniture, and printing company. From then until 1982, we successfully grew the business to become one of the largest in central Ohio, a serious competitor to the top company. We started with $3,000 and ended up with 27 employees. We worked with a lot of political industries and were fairly successful. I was featured in a couple of newspaper articles and landed on covers of magazines covering entrepreneurial ventures.

Having not really had business training, I was not aware of what companies do in bad times. During the period I started in business, times were relatively good. By the late '70s and early '80s, the oil embargoes and inflation had started to take their toll. By 1982, money that used to cost 5 percent on business loans had skyrocketed to 26 and 27 percent—the beginning of the end was near. I had made the big mistake of growing the business in bad times instead of slowing down the business. I never understood the value of cutting back on the business. I reasoned that if you continue to grow, you can outpace anything. However, our growth outpaced our ability to capitalize the business. In 1982, I was working for free to feed 27 families.

I closed the business in 1982, filed corporate bankruptcy, and went to work for Continental Office Furniture and Supply, my previous competitor. I quickly became their government affairs/government sales manager, also in charge of some of their lobbying efforts. We successfully grew the business up from about $100,000 in revenues to about $20 million in revenues within a year and took Continental into the government marketplace for the first time. I was there from 1982 until about 1988. Another division of Continental doing business with the state came under a great deal of news media scrutiny. That scrutiny made it increasingly difficult for me to do my job and I decided to move on.

From there I started up my own consulting business, called Access Ohio. There are two types of lobbyists in Ohio: legislative lobbyists and executive agency lobbyists. I was the latter. The position is little more than a glorified registered sales person who helps corporations do business with the government. During that tenure, I represented a lot of corporate America; my most notable client was Motorola. I was growing my business successfully.

During the time that I was growing Access Ohio, my stepdaughter developed insulin-dependent diabetes at about age 11. Because I worked out of my home, I essentially ended up being the caregiver for both daughters. By 1992, my marriage was buckling under the pressure of various problems and I filed for divorce. I received custody of my daughter and fought for custody of my step-daughter. The cost and confusion of the divorce took a tremendous toll on my business and I shut it down in 1994. I spent the next two years as a stay-at-home dad, hoping to find some calm in the chaos of the divorce by being a good parent to my daughters. Small successes like learning to make mac and cheese were very important in regaining my strength to return to the business world. The divorce was finally settled in 1997 and my daughter Jessica continues to live with me.

I didn't realize it until later, but I've done the same thing with my daughter that my mother did with me. From the time my daughter was born until she was a senior in high school, we did not have cable TV or Nintendo. But what she has had are art lessons, dance lessons, and music lessons. She has a library of the books she's read and collected that would embarrass a scholar. I always tried to make available to her the same things that were available to me. If you wanted some paint brushes and some paints, you could have them. If you wanted a new coat to show off with, the answer was no because we didn't have the money.

In 1996 I went back to work to become executive director of K9 Companions for Independence, a group started by Charles Schultz. We provided well-trained dogs to help children with disabilities. While I'd always been fairly free moving around Columbus, that was the first time I was involved directly with children with difficulties and it proved a very worthwhile experience. Watching young people coping with issues and then seeing the impact that a dog had on their life was eye opening.

My nature is to challenge, probe, push, hit, and scream, "Why can't we do it better? bigger? faster?" I learned some important things at K9 Companions. First, how important assistance can be to children and how difficult it is to provide that help. And second, with every organization, the politics of getting something done are more significant, more important, and more of an obstacle than actually getting it done. My business and political backgrounds began to converge in a way that I could not have predicted.

Back when I was involved with Office Works, I had learned the balance sheet basics of buying and selling and how to grow a business. I also learned what it looked and felt like when a business fails. My two years at the Attorney General's office allowed me to understand the convergence of how government and business work together. As the business manager there, I dealt with a lot of corporate vendors from the perspective of the government.

I've had some experience in government, in political campaigns, and in nonprofit organizations. I've had some experience running my own businesses, sitting on some civic boards, and acting as president of civic associations. All of these began to culminate into a set of unrelated experiences that would come to bear fruit as ECOT developed. If you look at ECOT, it in fact represents all those elements. It is a nonprofit company that acts like a business. It is a system for delivering to children who really need it. It is an ongoing campaign to overcome media and political obstacles. I need to know the finances of a business owner, have the heart of a nonprofit person, and demonstrate the tolerance to report to a government agency.

One of my favorite books is called *Finite and Infinite Games,* by James P. Carse, a Jesuit priest. I tell my daughter, "When you get a book, get our your marker or your pen, tear out the pages, dog-ear the pages, and highlight it. It's there to be used, not to look pretty." That book happens to have every sentence underlined. It's one of those books that I've carried around for years.

What the author writes about are two types of people:

- People who play in a finite world of goals and achievement measured by where they live and what they own and how they are portrayed

- The infinite player who exists only to keep the game alive

All that goes before and after those definitions is to keep the game in play. I remember playing basketball with my brothers when we were growing up. We'd go out and play basketball, 21, but we could never get the game over because when we got close, we would extend the game to 41 and then to 51. Instead of saying, "We won and the score was…," our question was, "Could we stay out until the sun goes down playing the same basketball game?" We couldn't tolerate having somebody win; we had to keep the game alive. I really believe in that philosophy. My passion is not about "What do I accumulate along the way?" or "When does it stop and I get my plaque?" When the game stops and I can't keep playing or keep the game alive, I have no purpose.

My struggle, in a very real sense, is to keep the game alive every day. As you learn of the struggles with ECOT, you will see that without that attitude we would have failed. While we have some very talented people and ideas, our ability to keep the game alive is what has made us successful—not what we've accomplished, but what we are doing to look over the next problem. We always looked forward to an obstacle instead of back at our last success. I've applied the ability I got from my mother to ECOT, "Let's keep the game alive. Let's go over the next hill. If we stop to take a rest, then we die." In that light, the infinite games play a role in the way we play ECOT. We are there to keep the game alive for the students.

Graduate Profile:
ANGIE

Angie's goal is simple: to go wherever God leads her. Whenever she has a difficult choice to make, she prays for God's guidance and her path becomes clear. Her path right now is taking her to Indiana Bible College in the fall.

Angie feels sad for adults who continue to behave as children, only to find themselves in prison or dead as a result of their behavior. She knows that the public school environment that she left to come to ECOT was full of opportunities to make bad decisions. It was only through the support of a religious community that she found the personal strength to stand up to the drug culture at her school.

The first two years of high school for Angie were at Lakewood High School in a nice suburb of Cleveland, a neat, clean, orderly, and disciplined environment. To Angie, it was socially boring. Her father was moving back to Puerto Rico. Angie then transferred back to a high school in the Cleveland Public School District, where her mother lived. She was excited to be around her old friends who knew how to have fun. Angie finished her junior year at this school, after turning away from the bad influences that she had initially thought would make for an exciting high school experience.

With that excitement, however, came chaos. During two recent visits to this school, she reported that nothing had improved. The halls were crowded and crazy, with people constantly pushing and starting fights. The security officers had limited ability to keep the peace, provoking disrespectful behavior from anyone they attempted to control.

Angie began twelfth grade with some serious asthma attacks that landed her in the hospital. She didn't see any way she could catch up her missed classes until a friend told her about ECOT. Her initial impression was that it was too good to be true and for a while it was—her computer didn't work until the end of January. When she began to understand how much work she would have to do by June to graduate, she was overwhelmed. But her teachers and advisors were understanding and worked hard to help her complete the year.

Angie was the valedictorian of her class, but didn't receive her diploma for another month. She worked nonstop to finish her work and graduate. When her diploma arrived, she broke down into tears of pride. These tears were different from the tears she had shed just a few months earlier when she was sure she would never graduate.

Angie looks back on those seven months of wall-to-wall work as the most important seven months of her education so far. She says she learned more during those months than in all of the years of school before ECOT. She couldn't just show up at school and look over someone's shoulder to finish her homework. ECOT built her confidence in herself and helped her learn that she can accomplish anything if she tries. Whatever God has in store for her, Angie is ready.

3

THE TWO-MILLION DOLLAR QUESTION

"ECOT is an advantage if you want to grow up

and become independent.

This is your future ahead of you."

Angela Feliciano, ECOT Class of '01

My father's role in my life was no less special than my mother's, just different. Coming from a family of 10 kids, including eight boys who all were in the war, there wasn't a lot of room for excuses. He's a wonderful, very traditional, a-man-is-a-man, don't-let-anyone-see-you-cry type of fellow. However, about 15 years ago when his grandkids started showing up, they taught him how to say "I love you," and how to hug them. He's always been the backbone, get up, dust-yourself-off, and keep-going influence in my life.

My life has had several major catastrophic events in it. From my brother's death to my business failure and bankruptcy to my divorce, my dad has always been the one to say, "Get up. Dust yourself off. This is just a practice field for the big game." I didn't know then what he was saying at the time, until one day ECOT showed up and all the lessons resulting from those failures were needed.

When I took my corporation through bankruptcy in 1982, my parents had two different takes on it. My dad said, "Okay. That's practice so you'll now know that you learn more from going out of business than going in business. You've got your real-world Masters by going into business, now you get your real-world Ph.D. by going out of business. The next time, you'll see the warning signs or at least you'll be more attuned to what the health of the business is. Dust it off. If there's a purpose, there's a way." I left this experience with a clearer vision of what a business really is: an entity that can fail.

My mother's reaction was different. "You know, Billy, I always thought you'd be number one," she said with her predictable sense of humor. "I'm so proud of you. It was the biggest bankruptcy in the county this month." She always knew I could be the best! Even though I knew that the business was a victim of a down economic cycle and that I had held on longer than most, I still needed these insights from both my parents to help me heal psychologically. I had suffered disappointments and tragedies in my life, but this was my first failure and it hurt. I was out of the game.

After my parting company with K9 Companions, I accepted a sales job to pay the bills and give me the freedom to continue to raise my daughter. That job didn't challenge me in the way that I discovered I was ready for again. The entrepreneurial spirit was stirring and the game had to continue. I didn't yet know which ball I would pick up at that point, but I had been on the bench for two years, very much against my character. I had to make up for lost time.

During my Access Ohio years, I had done some work with Columbus Public Schools on the school reassignment plan (aka the busing plan). At the same time, I had been a consultant for Motorola and some other high-tech companies. Without realizing it, I had enough dangerous knowledge that technology existed. I gained a belief from Motorola, one of the most brilliant technology companies in the world, that if you can dream it, it can happen. But, at the same time, this pioneering company was one of the first to move a plant overseas because of a lack of qualified workers in the U.S. This didn't sit well with me. Why couldn't the United States system of education produce more than enough qualified workers?

I started reading more and more in the newspaper about Columbus Public Schools and worked for two candidates for the school board. I started to see what wasn't working in the public schools and began believing that technology could enhance the problem-solving process. The predetermined mindset that technology could be part of the solution was already there. If I didn't know that, if I didn't believe that, I could never have started ECOT. I also believed in the dangers of technology. Technology alone wasn't the solution. It was simply another tool. It's a power tool instead of a hand tool, nothing more. It will never be anything more than that, but power tools do things a little bit faster, safer, cheaper, and better than hand tools.

This idea that technology was a key to addressing the problems with public education occurred to me when an associate of mine and

I were active on one of the school board campaigns. He was active at West High School and I was active at Bishop Ready. We were putting out yard signs and became involved in school politics a little. His son and my daughter, whose birthdays are two days apart, pretty much grew up together. He went through a divorce and I went through a divorce, and our kids became surrogate brother and sister. Watching our children in these educational systems also drew us into the conversations that later proved to be the beginning of ECOT.

He had some lingering faith in the Columbus Public School system but I believed that it was a dismal failure because of results as measured by benchmarks such as graduation rates, literacy rates, and college acceptance rates. No business could suffer results that any school in Columbus Public delivers and not be driven out of business. You would not continue as the president of a company with those results for very long. Yet, in the traditional public schools, we create a self-feeding mechanism that allows you to not only stay forever but get promoted and paid beyond your worth by simply surviving. My friend and I would occasionally meet for coffee. We were talking about this charter school legislation we had begun to read about in the paper. "What's this charter school thing?" That was the question that started everything.

My mind and our conversations went straight to the business side of the solution first, before going to curriculum. The way I saw it, if you've got a good curriculum but the business isn't working, you're out of business. On the other hand, if you've got a good business and the curriculum is failing, you get another curriculum. Suppliers of educational services are everywhere. I had no anxiety about what we were going to teach the children. That was the easier part, or rather, the part of the puzzle that could be solved. The hard part was how to run this business of a charter school on about half the money that other schools receive and with no ability to raise capital. That was the problem to be solved.

Mike Bradley was an old acquaintance who would sometimes stop by the Waffle House, a coffee shop on Wilson Road. As his long career in business finance had earned him a reputation of being very savvy, I wanted his opinion of my fledgling idea. At this point, the idea had taken the form of providing an alternative to homeschooling. I knew that there was a growing population of homeschooling families and many were continuing to search for or build their own curricula. Some were paying monthly fees to curriculum providers. I felt that a charter school that delivered free electronic curriculum to these children and provided certificated teachers to supervise their work would be a big hit.

One evening I bounced my idea off Mike. His response was clear and succinct, "It won't work." I argued. He remained firm in his position. "No business can succeed without capital and they haven't left you any windows open wide enough for a fly to get in." Capital is the base and foundation on which a business is built. It's no different from a house. Before we put the framework up, we'd better have a good foundation. As I described to him everything that had to be done to make this work, his mathematical mind went haywire. I remember some choice adjectives that were designed to convince me I was nuts and that there were more sound business plans waiting to be developed.

But I had my mind stuck on the notion that children needed an opportunity for a better education and that technology was somehow the key. I challenged Mike, "So tell me how I get the capital. If I need capital, you're the expert, tell me what I have to do." His response was that if I was going to do it anyway, he knew some bootstrapping techniques, generally employed by start-up entrepreneurs, usually unsuccessfully. However, there are some start-ups, albeit very few, that are able to pull it off without having a chunk of dough up front in the form of capital.

Mike gave me the Business Finance 101 class (which we will

offer someday at ECOT) on a placemat. He is now a recognized lec-turer and expert on start-up charter school financing. It is worth repeating here because you will understand better what we had to do first. On top of that, it's information I believe everyone needs to know. There are only four sources of capital funding available to any business. We needed to eliminate the ones that were not available to us. Using low-level deductive logic, we would arrive at the ones that are left. Then we could focus on those sources and not waste time on the others.

The four sources of capital funding are

• Owner's infusion of cash in various formats (debt, equity)

• Long-term borrowing (over one year)

• Trade payables

• Surpluses retained in the business

That's all there are. You can search all four corners of the earth, but that's it. Let's look at them one at a time:

Owner's Infusion of Cash

For-profit corporations can receive cash from their stockholders as equity (purchasing stock) or debt (providing loans.) Nonprofit corporations have no stockholders but can accept cash as debt or donations. The amount of money I had to infuse into this corpora-tion was a lot to me, but amounted to a bee sting on a bull. It would have been equivalent to a $50 down payment on a $20,000 car. I did put in all I had as a short-term loan during the start-up period, before we received funds from the Ohio Department of Education. It didn't go very far.

Long-Term Borrowing

Couldn't do it. Government said so. The one exception is leasing, which can perform the same function as borrowing to a certain extent. Typically, leases are shorter term than long-term loans extended to businesses. A lease might be three years, four maybe, five if you're lucky, versus long-term borrowing that might extend seven, ten, or fifteen years. Leasing provides a better-than-nothing contribution to capital, but it is not as good as long-term borrowing. A new exception to this rule is a fund the state government has established for buildings.

Trade Payables

This is what happens when one business sells another business a good or service and doesn't ask for the money at the time of the sale. A payable is created on the books of the purchasing company. These are not technically capital for accounting purposes, although they function as such. Some expenses that accrue become permanent capital built into the business, such as the start-up payroll that doesn't have to be paid for three weeks. It just keeps rolling over.

Trade Payables are available to most businesses although the extent of them is not known until the business gets rolling. Some terms are 15 days, 30 days, or 60 days. Some industries, like gift shops, can take delivery on merchandise in March and not pay until next Christmas. This was going to be our main hope for locating capital.

Surpluses Retained in the Business

With a start-up, there are no surpluses until the business passes break-even, which may not be immediately. Once there are surpluses, it is necessary to retain them if you want to replace the dwindling capital base caused by repayment of initial sources of capital like leases and payables. Keeping the capital base strong is essential to the ongoing stability of any company.

After my refresher course from Mike, I realized that our only sources of capital would be:

- around $100,000 cash

- trade payables

- equipment leases

- a $50,000 start-up grant from the United States Department of Education

I disappeared for a while to figure things out and attended several seminars offered by the Ohio Department of Education to guide us through the process of applying for a charter.

I then began writing the application for the charter. We waited until the exact last minute to turn it in to qualify for the 2000/2001 school year. We knew the concept was so revolutionary that we would need a "protected" year of operation to establish our market presence before other schools formed. If we turned in the application too early, it might give other groups the formula that we had worked so hard to arrive at.

This is the phase that entrepreneurs go through when they have to consider carefully who knows what about the idea and when to release it to the public. It isn't always rational but more a part of the game to get to the treasure first with the right solution. Once the business is up and running, the feeling passes and the next phase is to make sure as many people as possible know what you are doing so that they can do business with you.

Different staff members at the Ohio Department of Education turned a cold shoulder to us and we sensed that our application would not be approved. So, just before the deadline to withdraw applications, we did. We then sent it to Tom Baker, superintendent of the Lucas County Educational Service Center, the original chartering organization in Ohio, which I will tell you about later. Tom saw the uniqueness of our idea immediately. He is an entrepreneur himself, bringing creative education services to northwest Ohio school districts. The preliminary application was approved in February 2000 and we received our charter in early April. We had a lot of work ahead of us.

I began to formulate the various solutions to make this school happen. When I was pretty sure I had identified all the key ingredients, we set out to find vendors. The biggest one, of course, was the electronic infrastructure of the school. There wasn't another one like it in existence, so I had to approach a company ready to think as no company had before. I picked Xerox. Years before, I had worked for them for a short time and discovered that they are innovators rather than followers. I had kept in touch with John Mirosavich, an executive at Xerox. After an initial conversation, John really went to bat and helped champion the idea of electronic education.

Mike, John, and I flew to Chicago for a marathon meeting with a few dozen top innovators and business people at Xerox. We had one goal for that meeting—trade credit. We knew they could do the job and we knew they would have to do it before we could pay them. They were going to have to like the idea so much that they would come in as a capital partner, providing us the trade credit we needed to make our idea happen, a mere 2 million dollars.

They saw the power of the model immediately and knew that if they didn't come on board, someone else would and they would miss the opportunity to be at the top of the leader board in the next greatest application of the technology revolution. As a result of that meeting, we had a school. Mike was scratching his head as we left that meeting. "How'd you do that? On a handshake, no less!"

Government officials love to talk about public/private partnerships. This was the purest example and the best application I could have imagined. It was a win/win/win. Xerox would position themselves as the innovators of the first K–12 Intranet secure server. We would get one of the best corporations in the world behind us. And the children of Ohio would gain access to education in ways never before thought possible.

Once Xerox was in, it was hard for others not to come along. It certainly would have been easier to have start-up capital in the form of cash to work with. The conversations with the vendors are a little longer when you explain that the sale they just made will not be paid for several months. Compaq signed on as our computer supplier. Information Leasing Corporation of Cincinnati provided the capital for the leases on the computers. We arranged other trade payables as we could not wait any longer: phone system, furniture, copy machine, and other necessary equipment.

We had our charter and our capital. Next we needed staff, curriculum, facilities, computers, and marketing. And of course we were going to need students. It was an exhilarating and thoroughly exhausting time.

Graduate Profile:

JACKIE

Jackie was eight years old when her parents divorced. Her mother wanted to start a new life at least a few hours away from their home in Ontario, Canada. She and Jackie found a home in Delaware County where Jackie joined 4H and spent all of her free time with her new horses. She traveled within Ohio to fox hunts and shows. She became president of her 4H Club, enjoying both the social and leadership opportunities it gave her.

Jackie's mother had often suggested home schooling. It wasn't that she disliked the education Jackie was getting in public school. She just thought it would be good for her to have more individual attention. Jackie was getting mostly Bs. As a normal teenage girl, however, spending more time with her mother was not on her wish list.

At the end of tenth grade, Jackie came home with the news that every mother fears: Jackie was pregnant. This began an understandably tense time between the two of them that ended with the decision to try home-schooling for eleventh grade. Jackie realized that by becoming pregnant she had given up her power to avoid homeschooling and still graduate on time. She planned on putting her baby up for adoption and selected a homeschooling curriculum.

The homeschooling curriculum arrived and was not what Jackie expected. She didn't agree with the conservative bias of the material, which made it difficult for her to take it seriously. As her pregnancy progressed, she was dealing with the emotional and physical changes that accompany most pregnancies. Her mom was there to help answer some questions with her schoolwork, but most of the time Jackie felt pretty much on her own.

The baby arrived in March of her junior year. Critical delays in the adoption process gave her time to bond with the baby and Jackie found it impossible to give up her daughter. With a baby to care for, schoolwork was harder and harder to make time for. Jackie ended up finishing her junior year late in the fall of 2000, after she had enrolled in ECOT for her senior year. She was quite happy that the start-up problems we experienced caused ECOT to postpone sending her a computer and assigning her the coursework. Our delay allowed her just enough time to finish her home-schooling curriculum from the previous year.

When Jackie actually started her coursework with ECOT, she was thrilled. She had teachers again! She found that her relationships with them were different from any she had ever formed with teachers at her public schools. Thinking back, she estimated the amount of individual time our teachers averaged with her at 10 minutes a day, but that was 10 more minutes than any teacher had given her individually in the past. It made all the difference. Jackie went from a B student to an A student, which was important to her as she had her sights set on and was successfully admitted to Ohio Wesleyan University, a four-year liberal arts college with high admissions standards near her home.

Jackie has just finished her freshman year at OWU and feels as though she was well prepared for the rigorous curriculum there. She has noticed something very interesting about her experience so far. She is eager and able to develop one-on-one relationships with her professors, while her classmates tend to shy away from individual interaction with them. She thinks back to her experiences in high school classrooms where staying after to talk with the teachers was seen as kissing up by her peers and therefore never happened. Because of the private nature of the communication that ECOT students have with their teachers, they don't have to deal with this stigma. As a college student, Jackie is never confused or behind for long. She seeks out assistance and never feels shamed for doing so.

Jackie is majoring in art and psychology, planning to attend college straight through to her Ph.D. She sees herself in a career as a child psychologist with a specialty in art therapy. Her interest in this career began at home, meeting kids from all types of situations, as her mother is a foster care provider for Delaware County Children's Services. Jackie has seen firsthand the needs of a variety of children in her community. She currently works part-time as an aide in an independent living environment for mentally retarded adults. She chose this job as a way to gain experience in the field of social services and counseling.

Her daughter is now two years old, active, and healthy. She attends daycare while Jackie is in school. Jackie's mom and the baby's father fill in while Jackie is at work. Jackie sees the years passing quickly and knows that she has a short three years before she will be making educational choices for her own daughter. She already knows where she might like her daughter to go. And I will gladly deliver that computer myself.

4

THE CUSTOMER IS
ALWAYS RIGHT

"In traditional schools, every child is not getting the

education their parents want them to get.

We are such an education-based society,

there is no reason not to perfect it."

Jaclyn Cartier, ECOT Class of '01

As an entrepreneur, I am wired to receive a charge from a waiting market. Energy flows through the economy randomly and entrepreneurs are the receptors who channel that energy in businesses that serve those markets. A market is created when a willing seller and a willing buyer meet. Stated differently, a market is where a resource meets a need. The Associated Press has ranked the top 10 news stories of the '90s. Number one was the advent of Internet technology: the resource. Number two was the demise of our public education system: the need. Without knowing that they were related, I had been receiving these stimuli for years. As soon as both reached the same level, my entrepreneurial antennae caught the signal.

As the seeds of ECOT were planted, it became obvious that we weren't just starting a business. We were revolutionizing a 160-year-old institution—public education. We were attempting to change the core concepts about what education is and how it works. We were about to go up against the strongest unions, the most entrenched bureaucracies, the shakiest politicians, and everyone's collective memories. Could there possibly be a more insane thing to do?

Another notion about entrepreneurs is that it is highly unusual that only one entrepreneur will see the resource meet the need and, therefore, have a long protected time to nurture the idea. If the idea is worthy, it will happen simultaneously in several places at once. Different entrepreneurs will envision slightly different forms and the strongest will survive to carry the idea forward. Whether or not ECOT has found the single most viable formula to bring together technology and education remains to be seen. The market will answer that question. What is certain is that the need to improve public education is undeniable and the promise that technology holds to accomplish that goal is encouraging. The momentum of the idea of electronic education, only two years after its inception, is already proving unstoppable.

I would rather it not be one victor over other entrepreneurs but a shared victory. From that standpoint, the students will win. The graduates of the Class of '01 are all winners. They were able to use technology to finish their high school education in a way that no student before them in the United States could claim. As you continue to read their profiles, you will see that they are as different and as beautiful as snowflakes, each drifting toward his or her unique place in this world. There is no reason why, at the dawn of the 21st century, we can't deliver a dynamic, unique, excellent education to any student, anywhere, at any time, at whatever pace that student works, and regardless of the path the student needs to take.

We have a tendency in traditional thinking to believe that education stops and starts during certain time frames. From age 5 to 18; from 8:30 a.m. to 3:00 p.m.; from September to June. And certainly not on major holidays. Then you get a diploma or a degree and you're done. One of the advantages of e-education is that the students who learn through this kind of system automatically become lifelong learners. Learning will become a condition of living instead of an activity of living.

In an e-learning environment, education long-term is really the ability to navigate a library and to seek, search for, and acquire knowledge. The Internet has connected our world and our libraries. It has given us access to people and resources everywhere. And it also talks back to us in ways that libraries have never been able to do. It gives us motivation through connections to other people browsing in the same section of the library. In ECOT's online library, our students are taught to be noisy, not quiet. We are changing the dynamics of research, encouraging students to connect and share. Our children in school today will not remember what the quest for information was like before the world had this power to connect. Their comfort in connecting with other people as they learn and grow will shape their entire lives. They will rely on it throughout their careers.

E-schooling truly is where the advantage of business and tech-

nology can come to the forefront to help educators and teachers produce better and more resourceful students. It's being perceived,
however, as the irresistible force meeting the immovable object.
Clearly education today has become an immovable object.
Technology is taking education where it has not gone before. In
most settings, however, it is being used as not much more than an
expanded research library and a message sender. The e-schooling
revolution is allowing technology to be a delivery mechanism for
education, not just a fancy chalkboard.

The adoption of these strategies by K–12 learning environments
follows the eager acceptance of e-learning strategies by two other
centers of learning in our culture: colleges and corporations.
Colleges and universities have taken technology into every student's
educational experience. Each college class will have a Web site on the
college's server with assignments, help chats, resources, additional
readings, and e-mail to the professor. Homework is often submitted
electronically, even when the class meets in person daily.
Corporations are delivering more and more training through on-line
distance classes that adjust to the workers' scheduling needs and
learning styles. It makes sense that these delivery mechanisms are
trickling down into the primary and secondary education years, both
as efficient and effective strategies and as a way to prepare youngsters
for the world ahead of them.

This is a seminal opportunity to bring to the marketplace, halls
of government, civic and community leaders, and, most importantly, to parents the ability to understand, grasp, and adopt what will
become the school of the future. I really feel safe in this prediction:
In 20 years electronic education will be the first-choice alternative for
parents whose children do not work well within traditional schools.
Or better yet, to change the definition of what is now traditional to
be inclusive of more learning styles, more special needs, and more
scheduling conflicts. There is no reason why an e-learning system

like ECOT can't allow every child to succeed in a public education system for no more money that we currently spend. As technological efficiencies advance, very soon it will cost even less money.

As emotional as it sounds, we are legitimately advocates of our future. We do not see a future that should be wrought with conflict or extensive political debate. E-learning should and will eventually become a cooperative effort, a cooperative momentum, and a cooperative future with all educators working together. E-learning belongs everywhere, including within existing traditional school buildings.

The biggest point to make, and I can't make it strongly enough, is that this idea of K–12 e-schooling is going to change forever the way we deliver education. This is a paradigm shift no less extraordinary than the advent of the automobile or electricity. We're reversing the parent role, we're reversing the choice role, and we're taking education into a market-driven role. We have had some role confusion in public education for quite some time. Who, exactly, is the consumer? Several groups have tried to lay claim to this title:

- taxpayers, who pay the bill

- employers, who hire the graduates

- politicians, who hire the education providers

- teachers, who dedicate their lives to the children

- parents, who are legally responsible for the students

- students, who have no political or social standing in the process

- the bureaucracy itself, which must focus on self-preservation as its primary purpose

No matter which group we identify as the possible consumer, there is a common thread that binds. All of them were students at some point in their lives. Beyond that, many of them are now parents of students. Loving a child is arguably the deepest emotional bond that a person will form in his or her lifetime. This simple fact propels that role to the forefront when a person debates the education problems we have. There is no psychological way that a parent can care as deeply about someone else's education than their own child's. Even teachers who are parents will have greater emotional investment in their own children's education than in the education of their students.

Considering these simple truths, we can only conclude that parents are the true consumers with the true demand. When you give control back to the spender, the consumer, the parent, you are basically saying, let's change this idea to what turns the parent into a customer. In the current system, parents only have the power as voters and taxpayers to control, in general, the state of their education system. E-schooling, delivered in a public school system, enables parents to become true consumers of education services for their children.

That single dynamic will bring the walls of Jericho down. That single dynamic in 10 years will have a totally different-looking physical plant, an organizational model for school districts. The school districts that figure it out now will survive and thrive. The parents, aka voters, will continue to fund them and send their children there. Those districts that restrict choice to a one-size-fits-all education will find dwindling enrollment, shrinking tax bases, and dissatisfied customers.

I have talked about waiting markets as the motherlode for an entrepreneur. It became obvious to me on March 31, 2000, that parents were the consumers in this waiting market. They comprised not only a waiting market but an anxious market. They had been waiting for so long that they had given up hope, in many cases, that a supplier would come along to meet their need. They had been trying to consume educational services through the normal channels and it wasn't meeting their needs—the market was springing leaks everywhere. Ohio had been trying new approaches to allow parents some choice in their children's education but it wasn't enough. On that day our charter was granted and leaked to the media. It wasn't what we would have chosen, but we did learn that the market wasn't only waiting, it was anxious to the point of panic attacks.

Another piece of evidence that the market was not being served was the simple examination of the cost structure. Public education is free to parents. Yet record percentages of children drop out before reaching graduation. When a business puts out a sign and advertises their service as free but no one comes in, there is something wrong. If the service is free, why can't they give it away?

I haven't met a parent yet who wants his or her child to drop out of high school. Some may go along with it once their child becomes so adamant, belligerent, or unruly that it seems to be an easier road to take. The question to be asked is why the child adopted those behaviors. The public school systems seem to leave the responsibility for this at the curb. Get the students here and we'll educate them. Schools are not evangelical, in any sense of the word. When a child drops out, in many school districts there is no exit survey; no statistics are measured; no quality controls are changed to look for ways to prevent the next customer from taking their child and leaving. When we reflect that private business is not only concerned but obsessed with listening to their customers, we can see another reason why business influences will be very positive for education.

A new era is dawning with the advent of school choice. We've always had competition from Catholic schools and a few private schools. Now we have charter schools and limited school voucher programs. Public schools have formed magnet schools within their districts and opened up enrollment for students to shop within their district for schools that meet their needs. These options are minuscule compared to the revolution that is now happening. E-schooling will break down all the artificial walls limiting competition among schools. Schools will be held accountable for their results and parents will have real choices to make.

You will see the ubiquitous quality of technology redefine the word "school." What happens when the Internet gets faster, cheaper, and better? In 10 years, the cost of bandwidth, computing, and education will be so inexpensive that e-schooling can take place anywhere. Why send your children to a physical plant, to a school? That may be a choice, that might be part of it, and that might be some of the time. This trend will run right alongside the decentralization of all other aspects of our economy, also made possible by the availability of bandwidth.

For instance, the mentality that school starts at 8:00 a.m. and finishes at 3:00 p.m. is wrong. Studies show that high school students don't have the biological ability to even begin learning until 10:00 in the morning. High school students will study at midnight, if given a choice. If you put a computer in the home with glass walls and the occupants can't see that you're looking in and then you say, "Okay, go compute," high school kids go back on the computers at 11:00 at night after everyone else is in bed. If we look at where the demand is, when students want to study, how they want to study, and where they want to study, it looks less and less like traditional education and more like ECOT.

The central goal for the survival and viability of e-learning is how quickly we can help educate traditional school systems to see what we do and to be able to say, come look at us—let's do this together. Let's develop a market-driven model that satisfies parental choice. School districts will thrive with satisfied customers who choose their schools for their children, vote for their levies, and volunteer for their programs. With a greater focus on education, schools will also attract and keep teachers more easily.

Control of learning will become decentralized, with parents exercising their choice. This will be a positive shift giving control back to families and communities. The students will feel the impact of this shift and know that decisions are being made in their best interest, not in the interest of some bureaucrat in Columbus or Washington.

School districts will still focus their services on the bell curve children but will not have to leave behind any child. E-learning services will pipe in any conceivable program of learning that a child needs to succeed at a fraction of the cost that the district would spend to develop and deliver a program to a small number of students. Students will not feel ahead of or behind their peers as they complete courses of study individualized to their needs. They will no longer have to speed up or slow down to feel accepted socially.

The benefits of e-schooling are so powerful and all encompassing that they have done nothing but frighten the existing power structure in the public education bureaucracy. They don't see how e-schools fit into their model, because they don't. They don't see how to pay for it, because they don't like it. They can't open up a conversation about it because their minds immediately go to a day when they are no longer in control. They are absolutely right, and that is what is needed. The centralized control that they have enjoyed has diminished the market power of the parents to demand what their children need.

It is embarrassing to a school district to have a student drop out at age 16 and then come knocking on ECOT's door at age 21, asking to finish his high school education. Why didn't he knock on the door of the school that he left? Why can't that school district service his needs? What are we offering that is attractive to him?

The answer is that the school district can service his needs, if they want to. But the incentive has never been there to try. Until recently, this re-entry model was not possible. Now, every school district in the country can send a letter to their dropouts and tell them that at no cost to the student, on their own schedules and at their own pace, they could finish their high school education. The dropout rate is the most critical issue facing our public education system, but it is only the first of many problems that can be solved by e-learning.

A simple definition of insanity is the ability to repeat the same action and expect different results. Our public education system has been repeating the same actions for too long now and expecting different results. But when presented with a totally new demand-driven approach, they hide, fight, and manipulate. They are absolutely sure that their ways will someday produce different results. They may, but it won't be the results they are hoping for. They will lose more customers and more faith from the communities that they need to support them.

In one year as a school, ECOT became the largest school in Ohio, larger than one-third of the school districts. When a parent tells a school district, "I'm taking my child and going somewhere else," they are making the strongest statement possible about the condition of their schools. It is expected that those public servants who had enjoyed a protected monopoly for decades would react negatively to this. And they didn't disappoint us. They are scared that they will have to change their whole paradigm. My prediction is that they will be forced to change and that the children will be the beneficiaries because the customer is always right.

Graduate Profile:

SHANNON

It would be hard to name a type of public school that Shannon has not attended. As she thinks back through all her educational experiences, she can't point to any that were better than ECOT.

Her first experience in elementary school was in a public school in Akron. Intimidation by gangs had crept down to the lower grades and was so bad that the school was converted to a private academy. Shannon remembers going shopping for her uniforms. She didn't like them, but when she noticed that no one hassled her about her clothes any longer, uniforms made sense. Schoolmates had been beaten when they refused to turn over a nice jacket or a pair of shoes to a gang member.

Her father's career as a minister brought their family to Columbus when Shannon was in the fourth grade. She was back in a regular public school. A year later, another move landed her in a middle school in Gahanna, a wealthier neighborhood than she had ever lived in. She felt safe there but socially excluded as one of only three African-American children in her class.

The next move was the most traumatic. In Nashville, Tennessee, she found herself back in elementary school as a sixth-grader. How demeaning! What did she do to deserve this?

When Shannon moved on to middle school (again!) the next year, life was grand. In a racially diverse school, she was much more outgoing. She joined the National Honor Society and the cheerleading squad. She felt confident both academically and socially.

After eighth grade, Shannon's parents divorced and she moved back to Columbus with her mother and brothers. She attended Independence High School in the Columbus Public School district. During tenth grade, she was on track to graduate a year early. She recalls that her guidance counselor tried to dissuade her from moving that quickly. His argument was that she could take her time, have more fun, and make more friends if she graduated on schedule. Shannon already knew that she wanted to attend DeVry Institute of Technology and didn't see any reason to hang out in high school any longer than necessary.

One day her mom received an emergency phone call at her office on the other side of town. There was a bomb threat at Shannon's high school. She raced to the school to get Shannon and her brothers, panicked and afraid. Everyone was safe and the bomb threat had been just a threat, it seemed.

A couple of weeks later, about the time that their blood pressures were returning to normal, the phone rang again—another bomb threat at Shannon's school. Another chase across town to find her babies. Again they were safe, thankfully.

A few days later, the third phone call was too much. The tension and fear were starting to impact Shannon's schoolwork and her mom knew that Shannon was having trouble concentrating. As Shannon finished tenth grade, they learned about ECOT and made the decision to switch. Some of Shannon's friends were able to slough off the bomb threats as no big deal, but Shannon and her mother felt too much pressure.

Shannon had always been a good student and a responsible child. Studying at home gave her the opportunity to focus and excel. At the ECOT orientation, she heard that her goal of graduating early would not only be possible but supported. After waiting a month for her computer, Shannon was off and running. She had a great year, enjoyed wonderful relationships with her teachers, and felt very prepared when she arrived at DeVry.

Shannon is majoring in Business Administration and is on track to earn her Bachelor's degree at age 20. She loves her Psychology and Critical Thinking classes. She sees herself as having a world of opportunities ahead of her—she certainly has a world of experience behind her.

5

THE QUESTION OF SOCIALIZATION

"School is not the only place to socialize. It's not like I was snatched from the world and stuck at home."

Shannon Pounds, ECOT Class of '01

It seems to me that the more I study about culture, the less I know. The complexities of human culture are mind-boggling and compelling at the same time. Individual psychology is interesting enough by itself, but when people gather and combine their individual personalities into a group culture, the game becomes very interesting.

Culture is defined as a set of norms established by a group. These norms stem from common and negotiated values shared by the group. When students, teachers, parents, and administrators form a school, a culture is formed and norms are established. The assumption is that the school culture will hold learning as one of its core values. Conflicts arise when individuals perceive that other members of the group have abandoned one or more of the core values that define the group.

When today's leaders come together to make decisions about education issues, they have a mental image of the culture of education. It will look amazingly like the education they experienced when they were young, although it may have been adjusted due to their experiences as parents in the system. Unless they are a teacher or administrator in a school building, however, they will not have an accurate reading on the current culture that exists today in our various schools.

Lawmakers have questioned the assumption that learning has continued to be one of the core values present in the public school culture in recent years. The increasing requirements of standardized testing by states and the federal government is evidence that they do not automatically trust the culture to keep this value in the forefront. They want proof that it exists and is effective.

As they point to solutions to bring the system back into balance, they often pick isolated strategies from their youth and demand that they be reinstalled. The argument over school prayer is an example of a cultural norm that existed when many of today's leaders were youths. Rituals, whether religious in origin or not, form a backbone for all cultures and provide continuity and comfort to those individuals in that culture. Our emphasis on team sports and the events that support them is an example of a set of rituals that let people know they are in the right place.

When our communities send their children into the public school system and they come out without having learned the basic skills of reading and math, this creates a cultural conflict. The assumption that learning is happening in the schools is a reasonable one. When it doesn't happen, we are left to wonder what the culture of public education values instead. When teachers complete their degrees and enter the profession eager to teach but find themselves little more than highly paid hall monitors, they are personally devastated. When principals are more concerned with keeping guns out of their schools than keeping learning opportunities in, they have ceased to be cultural leaders helping the group to value learning.

It has reached the point in almost all school districts where education has taken second place to police work. Indeed, the local police forces have been invited into the school buildings to offer their presence and specialized training to minimize the gang activity, violence, and personal safety threats to teachers and students. Students must constantly adjust their behavior to minimize the possibility of physical harm and psychological abuse.

Those who choose not to participate in the drug and gang culture have extraordinary personal strength and family or church support. It is not the type of skill set that we might expect any adult to have, let alone a developing teen with all the social insecurities of growing up. The middle school and high school years are emotionally volatile years to begin with. Students must grapple with their own challenges and try to get an education. Locked in a culture with exposure to self-destructive behaviors and fear-inducing situations is not a culture conducive to learning.

I imagine that most adults today believe that their own child-hoods were packed full of dangerous behavior and opportunities for crossing the lines. That's what children do—they test limits and determine their own capacity to take risks and survive. A dangerous mindset that we can adopt is that the kids today aren't doing anything we didn't do. Psychologically, that may be true. But the lines have moved and the tools of self-destruction are more lethal. We did not have an AIDS virus, semiautomatic weapons, crack cocaine, and gang initiations.

As school districts, administrators, and teachers are forced to address these acute dangers, their attention is naturally drawn away from their presumed purpose of education. Those students who are interested in getting an education are forced to fight for attention with troublemakers who drain the system of time and resources. They often find ways out of the system through moving to better school districts, private schools, magnet schools or charter schools, or homeschooling.

Those children who do find alternative education sources leave behind those with fewer resources, weak family support, or a lack of ingenuity to struggle within the system. Those children who are truly interested in learning are given fewer opportunities to learn. Classes are distracted by those children who do not want to be there. Children are easily lured away from school by friends or jobs. Truancy and dropout rates are skyrocketing in many districts. The cultural bond formed by the school is no longer strong enough to overcome the fact that the children do not feel they are in the right place. So they leave.

A child in public school today can walk away from that building after signing in, and nobody cares; it's so easy to make the decision to not attend school. Attendance at school is the start. If you don't show up, you can't be educated. Ask any principal in any high school in America, "If the child shows up every day, I will educate them."

Now we have a business where children, for whatever reason, can leave school and drop out. Once a child has made that decision and is a couple of months behind, it's difficult to go back.

Ever since parents have been routinely sending their children to a school building 180 days a year, the world has assumed that school is the environment where the child is "socialized." Learning the rules of social engagement is certainly important for success in our world. If a culture and its accompanying norms form wherever people gather, however, we can assume that a school building is only one of many social settings where children will need to understand the rules as they get older. There are rules that will transfer and rules that will not. Learning to line up to go to the bathroom is a skill that comes in handy at concerts; sitting cross-legged in a circle with your hands folded would look a little silly in a corporate board room.

It is not the absolute rules that a child must learn but the integration of those rules into a culture. And, more importantly, the adaptation of those rules as they move among different cultures: from school to work to church to community events to family settings. The other 180 days of the year, the student is negotiating these other cultures. Even on school days, only one-third of the time children are awake is spent in the school environment.

As far as where children receive their socialization, I would argue that during the 15 percent of their time that students spend in school they are learning to be in school. During the 85 percent of their time that students spend out of school, they are learning to be in the world that they will inhabit once they are "done" with school. To presume that a child who is homeschooled or learning through a distance learning course will not have the benefit of the socialization that occurs in school is true.

Before we dismiss this fact as a drawback, two things are important to consider. First, the student who is concentrating their academic learning time separately from socialization activities is more efficient at learning. This allows more time in a student's life to participate in activities that lead to healthy socialization, like community service activities, sports, time with friends and family, participation in scouts, and attending church. Second, there is a strong assumption that the socialization available from a school setting is positive and healthy for the child.

The world is now asking whether the socialization available through public education is positive or negative to the child. The stories of several of the kids that ECOT taught give us a peephole into the worlds that they or their parents wanted out of. Is it necessary that to become a successful adult a teenager must submit to self-destructive behavior in order to have friends and be protected from gang violence? It's such a ridiculous notion that I feel ashamed that we have put so many of our young people in this position.

The current education industry is often eager to blame the parents for these challenges. Some children are not sent to school with adequate nutrition, appropriate parental nurturing, or enough sleep. They are witnesses to domestic violence, drug use at home, and all the other ills that society can serve up. We can go around and around about society's ills that are dumped on the schools, but who taught the parents who are now sending these ill-equipped children to school? There is some shared responsibility here, at the very least.

The students who have found their way to ECOT are representative of the overall population of students in public schools. Their lives are fluid. They move, change custodial parents, and don't get too attached to any one situation. Of the students who responded to our surveys, 70 percent qualify for free or reduced-cost lunch programs. The economic stability of these households is always in question. We had one of our computers show up in a pawn shop, presumably the only asset left to pawn to fix the next crisis for that parent.

Virtually every social crisis present today is represented in our student body. And it should be. The definition of public education is to make education available to the public. A child who has been orphaned or abused is no less deserving of a good education than one with two living, loving parents. In fact, the abused child will probably need the education more. A child who has children or who is struggling with a fatal disease or who suffers from the chronic symptoms of fetal alcohol syndrome needs education even more than a healthy, happy, unencumbered child.

We also have the children who have been literally abused by the social environment in their public school. One girl was stabbed in the stomach while at school and intimidated into not reporting the crime. Her mother accidentally walked in on her in the bath and saw the gangrene forming around the wound. We have three children who have been sexually assaulted by school personnel and knew no one would believe them. One child was raped by an older school-mate and her only way to school was on the same bus with her attacker.

When adults are traumatized by a situation either in their neighborhood, their workplace, or their family, they often have options to separate themselves from the fear and risk of a repeat attack. The education system does not always allow this remedy to children. Other students in the system are often aware of the potential threat to themselves as well. Most adults I know would not tolerate the constant fear and pressure that many of our young people live with every day of their lives. The cultural rules become survival, not growth; coping, not exploring. This is not a culture where the value of learning can thrive.

Having lived in a metropolitan area my entire life, I held a common belief that the suburbs and rural areas were immune to these types of problems in their schools. However, from the reports we are getting from students who have come to ECOT from 603 of the 611 school districts in Ohio, I couldn't have been more wrong. The intensity may not yet be as great, but the same problems are there. In some cases, the presence of affluence masks the issues or finds more effective solutions, but they are still there.

Much of the socialization of kids in the public schools is centered on promoting a few while punishing the many. Keep pushing them until they fail. It's the American way. Many kids will never buy into this death spiral approach to accomplishment. Then they are labeled as underachievers. They are rarely measured against the only measurement that truly matters, their own ability. Instead, they are measured against each other and some arbitrary benchmark of excellence that could never be reached.

ECOT is working hard not to join the ranks of schools with that image. We want the image that if you want to learn, learn, learn, you have all this information available and all these teachers available. You can have a one-on-one education. Your teacher can choose from curriculum that you want to learn, based on certain guidelines. We don't want to stop you from learning. If you can accelerate three grade levels, we want you to do that. The emphasis is on your advancement at the pace that allows you to learn.

We are serving all types of children who don't fit into the culture of the traditional school. One little boy reminds me of Doogie Howser. He tests at a twelfth-grade level; he's a third-grader. He can take high school math but lacks the maturity to sit in a high school classroom. We've also served a quadriplegic girl who is blind in one eye. The parents pleaded with us, "Please, teach our daughter." We didn't know how to do it at the time, but we figured it out. These are somebody's children and giving them the opportunity to do what they can honors their uniqueness as human beings.

We are experiencing an interesting dynamic at ECOT that will need to be researched over the years. As children are freed from the pressure of peer criticism and control and given direct access to their teachers and essential support from their parents, they seem to shed earlier social disabilities. The computer communication allows them to send and receive messages that don't carry the same psychological impact. They are not as sensitive to the possible judgment of others and they open up socially. Children who have not been able to "fit in" to the culture of public school for a variety of reasons may feel comfortable in an e-schooling environment. This builds their confidence to be able to socialize in other settings.

We are finding that much of learning is a private, quiet activity where the student interacts with their online curriculum or other materials. Other learning takes place as the students interact with teachers, students, and parents. We are also promoting the extensive use of field trips. We have an affiliated company called Learning Adventures whose sole purpose is to create field trips for families. In our first year, we organized 40 trips and over 100 the second year. This count does not include the field trips that parents organized themselves. Taking their skills out into the community with other ECOT students and parents is the true test of the student's ability to socialize and apply their classroom skills.

Legislators, political leaders, and teachers often ask me, sometimes critically and sometimes supportively, "What are you doing to provide socialization for your students?" One of the parents put it well, "Why look at art in a book when you can go to a museum to see art?" Does a culture promote learning by sitting children in a room for six hours dictated by time and bells and schedules and coursework? Is that really the way a person learns? Is it the way children learn? Well, they certainly do, but is that the best way to learn? I can't recall a time that I was not overjoyed over the prospect of a field trip when I was in school. If you look at the culture of learning, you have to ask yourself whether we have been doing it right in the first place. I don't know that we have.

With e-schooling, the culture of learning will be different, probably better. Children will be socialized and comfortable in an electronic culture, which will dominate most of their work environment in the future. They will have more time to interact with other humans face-to-face outside of their education environment, allowing a greater development of these skills apart from the competitive, pressured world of school. Thirty years ago, futurists were predicting that technology would be the engine of vast social change. E-schooling is a reaction to this change that is already occurring, not the catalyst of change.

Graduate Profile:
MANDI

Mandi didn't feel very well at graduation. It was a beautiful event and she was proud to be there, but when she saw the video she says she looked green! A few days later, the doctors at the local hospital confirmed that she had a reason to be green: Mandi had a dangerous kidney infection. Grateful to the doctors and nurses who cared for her, Mandi hopes to go into the medical field herself. After a beautiful experience several years earlier with hospice nurses who helped her grandfather come home from the hospital to die, Mandi would love to be a hospice nurse.

Mandi was born and raised in Whitehall, a suburb of Columbus. She has two siblings much older than herself, so was given the love and attention of an only child. School was a difficult place for her from the very beginning. She attended one of the four elementary schools in the Whitehall School District. By second grade, she was failing. Repeating the second grade only made official what she knew all along—she couldn't learn the way other kids did. Her mother fought for special education for her, but was repeatedly told that Mandi was too smart for special education. So Mandi struggled.

A large girl a year older than her classmates and still not keeping up academically, Mandi was the brunt of excessive teasing. It wasn't until ninth grade that a very special English teacher invited her to participate in a reading group with other children having trouble. Mandi was shocked to see that many of the same children who had teased her for nine years were also in this group. Her reading level was assessed at a sixth-grade level and this teacher worked diligently to help Mandi catch up.

Mandi had been looking forward to high school. She had hoped for a more active social life, fun parties and outings, and more freedom. What she found shocked her to her core. The children who had built their self-esteem around intimidating other children were joining gangs. The boys were in charge and the girls were possessions, often passed around sexually at parties as a way for the boys to gain status. Drugs were everywhere and use of them was expected if you were to be accepted socially. Mandi didn't want any part of this culture.

Mandi describes her parents as the kind of people you could tell anything to. She knew they loved her and would stand up for her through everything. But she couldn't tell them about the gangs and the drugs. She feared that they would confront the school and make a scene, bringing even more taunting her way. She wasn't able to change this environment by herself, and besides, some of the girls had it a lot worse than she did. Who was she to complain?

With her reading skills improving, Mandi was more comfortable with her school work although the social environment caused her to go to school in fear most days. She knew which kids brought knives and guns to school (or claimed they did), so she spent most of her time trying not to make waves.

Mandi's mother came to work for ECOT the day we opened our doors. When she began telling Mandi about her job, Mandi immediately asked to transfer. Her mother was initially shocked, having been kept in the dark about many of Mandi's experiences at school. She was proud of Mandi for hanging in there and doing so well in high school in spite of the pressure. When she heard Mandi's reasons for wanting to leave, she agreed instantly.

Mandi was one of the few students who knew what was going on behind the scenes at ECOT because her mother was working nonstop to help us get the school off the ground. Mandi's problems getting online continued throughout her entire year with us. She actually came to work with her mother toward the end of the year so that she could to sign on to a computer at the office and complete her work in time to graduate. She showed as much commitment and determination as any student in the Class of '01.

Putting aside computer problems, Mandi embraced her ECOT experience. She liked being responsible for getting herself to school. She found teachers who cared about her the way her ninth-grade English teacher had. She had the flexibility to work shifts on her job that other kids didn't want. She felt the self-paced curriculum was perfect for her because there are some subjects that she learns faster than others. And there was no one there to tease her for taking more time when she needed it.

6

LET THE TEACHERS TEACH

"It's hard to believe what high school girls

have to put up with these days.

It's like they are somebody's property."

Mandi Riebel, ECOT Class of '01

The needs of children are so interrelated that it is difficult to see where education stops and social services begin. As the grand gatherers of children in our society, educators have been asked to address every issue from childhood immunization to drug abuse prevention to child abuse intervention. Whenever a child advocacy group or a legislator concerned about the needs of children conceives of a program for helping children, the schools immediately become a target for implementation because that's where children gather.

An outbreak of meningitis in a small town in Ohio last year prompted lawmakers to propose a bill that would require every school to distribute literature to every student, informing them of the risks, preventions, and vaccination available. A signature of a parent would be required to make sure the schools had complied with this order. Would they increase the funding to schools to cover this cost? Probably not. Would they reduce the educational requirements to allow the teachers to spend time fulfilling this mandate? Absolutely not. And maybe the districts would have to do a mailing to students currently homeschooled in their district. This is important, after all, and all children should be protected.

If given the time and resources, most public health officials could come up with other distribution channels for making sure that families receive this information. A public service announcement carefully scheduled on a TV show popular with children or a direct mail piece to households with children might have the same or greater impact. A couple of well-placed ads in the local papers or an announcement at the Fourth of July fireworks display might grab everyone's attention as well. You might argue that advertising costs money and that the announcement at the fireworks display might detract from the festive atmosphere.

Well, thanks to Milton Friedman, we all know that "There is no such thing as a free lunch." What we don't know is the second half of his famous quote, "That is the sum of my economic theory. The rest is elaboration." So, with Dr. Friedman's permission, I will elaborate. When you pay your taxes and those tax dollars are sent to school systems to educate children, you get a certain number of units of education, let's say. When you then ask those school systems to provide services other than education and you send them no more money, you will get fewer units of education. It is very simple. Every time we ask a school system to solve a social problem, we are asking them to teach our children less.

As society grew in complexity at the same time that families and churches relinquished ownership of the management of many of the accompanying problems, government picked up the ball. Sometimes willingly, sometimes reluctantly. Each problem that landed a child in front of a judge required the government to devote resources through the juvenile justice system. Each problem that endangered the health and safety of a child engaged the child welfare agencies. As it became clear that some children were not getting proper nutrition at home, the government added childhood nutrition programs to make sure all children had the food they needed. Did you know that our federal government buys half of the baby formula sold in the U.S.? Many of those babies receiving that formula go on to be fed by reduced-cost or free lunches and breakfasts throughout their school years.

Since World War II, the delivery of social services through educational providers has been carried to the extreme. We have given the public schools the responsibility for providing breakfast, latchkey programs, extracurricular activities, social consulting, psychological consulting, health services, and crime prevention. Schools have become home, and home becomes a place where you eat one meal and sleep. And it isn't working. By giving educators these mandates, we have allowed them to develop the attitude that they know best for our children. They don't. To me, even the worst well-meaning parents will probably deliver more for a student than the best-intentioned educator. I don't believe that a large institutional school system can provide individually what a child needs on a day-to-day basis. Educators need to be freed up to educate our children—it is too much to ask that they raise them also. Test scores will get lower and lower as their attention is diverted from their primary responsibility, educating our children.

Public education can and does do a good job with a certain slice of the population that they serve. If a child is in the middle of the bell curve academically and doesn't have a lot of medical, emotional, or social problems and comes from a background with reasonable parenting, the child will succeed in public schools. The system is not a failure to those kids. The kids who get Bs and Cs are the ones who are easy to educate. When you go any number of degrees on both sides of the bell curve, that is where you find that public education fails miserably. Public educators can't possibly be successful when they try, given their mandate, to serve all children and be all things to them: parent, social worker, dietician, nurse, psychologist, and truant officer.

If you don't fit the one-size-fits-all concept of the bureaucratic school system, you've got real problems. Is the school system a failure? Yes, for half the children it's a failure; for half the kids, it's not. More importantly, we're creating a generation of children and a generation of parents who don't have a lot of options. What if I didn't have the $12,000 for private school for my stepdaughter after her insulin-dependent diabetes took her out of school so often that she fell far behind? There are kids who can't get the education they choose because that school simply can't afford to teach kids who can't afford to pay them. For half the world of parents in our country, there's no option. And I saw that firsthand.

We now have a tug of war between (1) the schools, which point out that more and more kids are arriving at school not ready to learn, or worse, not arriving at all; and (2) the parents, who point out that the schools are encroaching on their turf and taking too much of a role in their children's lives. The school's knee-jerk response is to ignore or expel children who are unreachable. The parent's knee-jerk response is to take their child out of the system and demand choice in educational opportunities. Left unchecked, these parallel responses will lead to the total demise of the public education system as we know it. I'm not prepared to say that that will be a bad thing. It's time for the education system to return to its core responsibility—educating children—and for parents to return to their core responsibility—raising children. Other mechanisms can be enhanced or established to support parents through other social problems that impact their ability to hold up their end of the bargain.

E-schooling holds the promise to become an effective facilitator of both goals—educating children and raising children in an environment that the parent chooses is in the best interest of the child. E-schooling also has the distinct characteristic of being able to carry targeted information directly to a student or parent for the least cost of any information distribution system in existence. In the case of the example discussed earlier of the public health threat of meningitis to students, let's look at how an e-schooling environment would be efficient at solving that problem.

Assume that the Center for Disease Control identifies high-risk geographic areas or high-risk age groups for that disease. Public health officials could contract with each school district using an e-schooling model. They would have instant connectivity to each student through bulletin boards or e-mail. They could also have public postings for parents in the same system. A chat session could be scheduled, hosted by a local health official to answer parents' questions. An e-mail or Web site response form could ensure that each family received the information. School personnel would not have to be involved, trained, or diverted from their normal duties. Permanent information could be posted in the student's resources to be accessed in case of an outbreak of the disease or in case the student needed to get further information. The efficiency and effectiveness of this system is light years beyond the print-the-form, distribute-the-form, collect-the-form system of yesteryear.

Similar to the way in which traditional schools have gathered students together in order to distribute information, e-schools will gather students. The difference is that the information distribution system does not rely on education professionals as messengers and students as mail carriers. Parents can receive information directly and at a time conducive to their work schedules and energy levels. Local PTAs often provide important information to parents, but what percentage of parents show up regularly at meetings? It is not logical to expect parents to gather for meetings.

On the other hand, parents will gather online. On the ECOT Web site, we opened up an e-group for parents to talk with each other. Although it was not hosted by an ECOT staff person, we did monitor the site. That session lit up the second it was available and was nonstop chat for months. The types of issues that they were helping each other with were diverse. We saw serious problems discussed and friendships forming among the parents. We were delighted to be able to provide this forum for parents to end their isolation in dealing with the very real issues of raising children today.

Distribution of critical information to parents through the Internet has to be one of the best uses of the technology available. So much information has flooded the Internet that it is difficult for a parent to know which information to trust. We see our role as gatekeepers of a secure server to allow verified information through so that parents can receive efficient information on demand. Instead of taking on the parenting role as educators, we see our system as able to give parents the resources they need to keep their role as parent very clear. We see it more as another service that we can provide to parents that they can take or not take, a service that is not mandatory. They can go to our Web sites and our internal communication and read up on a whole host of topics. The goal over the next couple of years is to have literally a library of resources for the parents that will help them with issues at home.

The saddest situation that we encounter, that any school encounters, occurs when a parent is not physically or emotionally present in a child's life. Every child needs to be loved by someone and it tugs at the heartstrings of every teacher in the country when they know that a child is emotionally on his or her own. Our teachers have had to learn to cope with this in their role with ECOT more than in their previous jobs. We have attracted many of these children and listened to their stories: from the children in foster care because their parents are in prison to the teenagers who have no one to support them and are living on their own, working full-time. Often these children have changed schools so many times, it is difficult to know where they stand academically and, often, they are behind their age cohorts.

The situation where a child is transient and served by various social service agencies is one where e-schooling holds potential to stabilize at least a portion of the child's life. If the education can go to the child, regardless of where the child is, the child can find some continuity in an otherwise turbulent life. This application of e-schooling is not as much a fix for social problems as an adaptation of the educational system to make sure that children caught up in problems they can't control have some predictability in their lives. It can serve as the eye of the hurricane for them.

Children who have crossed many lines and ended up facing the juvenile justice system are another group that the public education system finds difficult to serve. Many times their offense is grounds for a mandatory expulsion from their regular school and other schools are not close by or able to service them well. With e-schooling, solutions are available that were not available before.

The dilemma the juvenile court judge has is that by the time a young person appears in court, the train has already gone off the track. By that time the public schools by and large have washed their hands of the youth. The school went through one series after another of public school programs trying to fix the problem. When they finally wash their hands, a young person appears before the judge, who has very few options. He can incarcerate the youth, which he does not want to do as statistics show that is not the way to rehabilitate someone. He can set the youth loose on the street, although that is not a responsible decision. He can put the youth back with his or her family, although that sometimes is the problem. He's required to give the youth an education, but he can't send him back to public school as the law has expelled him. As soon as the juvenile judges heard of ECOT, they immediately saw a solution.

We began a program in Kenton, a rural county seat in Eastern Ohio, where Judge James S. Rapp had set up a learning center for kids who were expelled by the school system and had no options for learning. He was able to take a few dozen children who were otherwise not able to get an education as there were no alternatives. His goal was to effectively blend their juvenile court experience, their social services, and their educational experience under one focus. He invited us to provide the education solution to these children with the help of the social service agencies mandated with their care. Unfortunately, Judge Rapp was such an innovator and forward thinker that he was ahead of us and the pilot program failed. The idea is revolutionary and we are moving ahead with it to serve children who have been cast away by their public school system.

This was one of the most unfortunate examples of our anxious market being ready before we were. This program holds much promise for bringing educational services to children all over the state where no solutions existed before. The judge was so excited about the program that he was talking it up all over Ohio. Judges were calling us daily to try to get a similar program. It was a matter of too much too soon for us. Some of the areas were so remote that the bandwidth providers couldn't handle the excess activity from a center with not enough computers. These problems have been addressed with the rapidly improving technology and we are now ready to step back into this arena for the coming school year.

We have had so many requests to do just that, from job and family services groups, social service locations, pregnant teenagers' homes, and juvenile courts that I clearly see our future as allied with those organizations. This is an example of education services being delivered through the social service agencies rather than social services being delivered through the school settings. This solves many problems for the child and society. It isolates the issues that children are facing and gives them trained professionals to help. It takes the pressure off the school system to be all things to all children. And, most importantly, the children can have seamless educations regardless of where they find themselves living or receiving other services.

The agency staff would fulfill the role of the parent for these children. Social workers, case managers, case aids, and teaching aids could provide the care that they are trained to deliver. In situations where the child's behavior has been disruptive to the classroom environment, a trained social worker could work with that child to improve behavior while the child receives his or her education online. Various combinations of e-schooling, community service, incarceration, home confinement, and work releases have been discussed by various judges as a way to integrate the young person back into society and, maybe, eventually into traditional school.

Another avenue where e-schooling can help our children who are caught up in the social problems of today is in conjunction with what President George W. Bush calls faith-based initiatives. To simplify, a church looks around at their immediate community and asks, "How can we help?" Many already provide resources through the generosity of their members, but President's Bush's notion is to allow federal program dollars to make their way to these initiatives as an efficient delivery system.

Many churches already provide homework help or after-school tutoring in their buildings. E-schooling computers could be installed on site in targeted areas allowing children to have supervision in an individualized environment. If they have already shown difficulty in the traditional school building or have become a behavior problem for the school, a smaller environment might be very positive for them. The problem, of course, is that no church could afford to develop an entire curriculum and hire a teacher for just a few students. E-schooling can be delivered at no cost to the church other than the staff to supervise the students, which could be funded through the type of program that the president is proposing.

In terms of situations where there isn't effective parenting, we should take our school and our social services dollars and our family fix-it dollars and our job dollars right back to the faith-based initiative President Bush is talking about. Why shouldn't there be a school in the basement of every church to welcome children whom the education system is not prepared to embrace?

The technology now available enables education to go to the child, wherever the child is best served and most loved. Raising a healthy, happy child is a complicated formula in this turbulent world. But providing a good education is not the hard part. The education should be of the flexible variety ready to respond as the child's needs are discovered. If parents are ready and able to raise their child, they deserve the choice of a quality education for their child. If the parents are not able to care for their child, society cannot afford to abandon the educational needs of that child as it provides for his or her basic needs. Children who do not enjoy the blessings of capable parents need a strong education base as they move through life. They should not be left to shoulder the burden of a lower-quality education just because the school systems are unwilling to adjust to their needs.

Graduate Profile:

RICHARD

Richard's memory of his 14 years in the Columbus Public Schools was that his teachers passed him up. He was a good kid who was never seen in the principal's office, but found learning profoundly difficult. As a first-grader, he was diagnosed with Attention Deficit Disorder. He repeated first grade and his mother began her 10-year battle to get him tutors. After he repeated the ninth grade, he did get tutors...in tenth grade.

Richard was a big, strong, healthy kid who loved to play football and basketball. Still does. However, he was never eligible to try out for school teams because of his low grades. He understood that he couldn't learn, but he didn't think it was fair to punish him when the school couldn't pro-vide him with the help he needed. With five kids, two of whom were ADD, his family couldn't afford the high cost of private tutors.

Richard finally gave up and dropped out of school in eleventh grade. He got a job as a groundskeeper and took the pre-test for a Graduate Equivalency Diploma (G.E.D.). He failed it. He began thinking about night classes at the adult education center. One night he was watching the local news in Columbus with his family when a story aired about the opening of ECOT. He says they all looked at each other and then he went straight to his computer to check out our Web site. His mother called the next day and enrolled two of her children. Richard was an adult—he enrolled himself.

ECOT gave them two computers, so he and his brother shared one. His brother would do his schoolwork while Richard was at work. Richard would study in the evening when he got home. Their sister had a computer to herself. Richard was surprised at the difference between learning from a computer screen compared with reading from books. He found it much easier to concentrate and stay focused on a lesson, working one screen at a time. He had never been able to absorb lessons delivered by lectures, so this was very exciting to him. He also encountered, for the first time, teachers who acted more like tutors. This is how he needed to learn.

Richard had always enjoyed using the family computer for video games and chatting with his friends. His time at ECOT helped him build confidence in using the computer for many other activities. He also learned that his need to focus on very small pieces of things in order to learn them is exactly the type of skill needed to program computers. On his own, Richard began exploring the information technology world as a potential career path. He is enrolling at Columbus State Community College this fall to begin working toward an information technology degree.

Richard is happy his brother and youngest sister are attending ECOT. Another sister graduated from South High's 100th graduating class the same month that Richard graduated as part of ECOT's first graduating class. He is proud of his sister. He himself would have loved to walk across that stage that has been an important part of the culture of the south side of Columbus for 100 years.

Richard's family has been very important to him throughout his life.

He is now working at Wal-Mart and enjoys it tremendously due to the family atmosphere there. He has a wonderful boss and enjoys all his coworkers. He says they do cheers at the team meetings. I bet this makes up just a little for all the cheers he missed not being able to play sports for South High.

7

FOLLOW THE MONEY

"Give us a chance."

Richard A. Wolff, ECOT Class of '01

Entrepreneurs, by nature, don't mind obstacles to entering a business. If a piece is missing in the puzzle we are trying to put together, we don't object to the search to find it. The assumption is that it would be just as hard for the next guy on the trail to find it after us. If a business is too easy to start, we assume that the competition will be active and right on our tail. But I have to say that, even knowing that character trait of mine, the obstacles to understanding how and when we receive our payments from the state of Ohio has really tested my patience and that of the entire staff at ECOT. The funding of public education in Ohio (and other states) has been under a microscope for the last 20 years, as court challenges and legislative nightmares drag on. It is difficult to understand and, once you do understand, it is difficult to see the logic in it.

I have not completed an exhaustive survey of the funding mechanisms in other states, but it has become clear to me that funding is a problem across the country. Education is such a high expenditure for most states that it is hard to find a funding formula that satisfies everyone. With the advent of charter schools, the plot has thickened. As a charter school, our funding is even more interesting. The next chapter will go into more detail to help you understand the history of charter schools and how we fit into that development.

There are 611 school districts in Ohio, ranging from a few hundred students to over 60,000. ECOT, with 3,000 students, is bigger than one-third of the school districts in Ohio. It is the single largest school at each of the three levels: elementary, middle, and high school. It is the largest K–12 combined school. Most other public schools that were started under the charter school law have fewer than 150 students.

Each school district elects a school board, which then hires a superintendent. The superintendent recommends the school principals and other district staff. Each principal staffs his or her school. The school board can go to the voters in their district for property tax and school district-specific income tax levies. They can also ask the voters' permission to issue bonds for capital improvements. The various decisions of the 611 boards and the voters in their districts have resulted in revenue to the districts ranging from around $1,000 to over $15,000 per student. Admittedly, it is a touch more expensive to provide education in the metropolitan areas, but that doesn't account for a $14,000 discrepancy in spending on education. This leaves the quality of education in the state highly variable, depending upon which district a child lives in.

The state collects money in the form of income tax and a small amount left over from lottery proceeds that goes to the schools. From that amount collected, each student receives a foundation amount based on a formula. The basic amount is $4,814 for the 2001–2002 school year. To give you some perspective, Michigan has changed their funding to be based on sales tax and provides a $6,000 basic amount per student. Ohio has been under a court order to fix the problem here for several years but has yet to install a solution agreeable to everyone. The state also provides money for school buildings and is currently distributing funds based on need. Some of the poorer districts are receiving long overdue help with some very embarrassing structural problems in their school buildings.

Ohio has a State Board of Education, half of which is elected directly by the voters and half of which is appointed by the governor. They hire a state superintendent of schools and approve overall education policy based on statutory mandates passed by the legislature. The superintendent supervises the Ohio Department of Education (ODE). Here is an example of their power: The legislature says that the state education department shall implement a consistent program for fire safety. Their goal is to coordinate with all the districts to see that they are in compliance and help them get assistance to develop it. This type of policy is usually reactive. It could have started because a school burned down and a child died, causing the legislature to react by passing a law. The state department of education provides consistency in these types of policies so that each district does not have to spend resources to develop their own policies.

Their main job, however, is to write checks to the local districts to distribute the state tax dollars and the federal grant money that comes to the state and to the districts. So, to add it up, each school district receives money from four main sources:

1. State income tax

2. School district specific income and/or property tax

3. State facilities improvement funds

4. Federal grants for education

The important thing to remember is that the different amounts spent on each student from district to district can be up to three times more than the district next door.

Responding to a mandate from the legislature, the state board of education established an Office of School Options designed to help districts provide more choices for parents than traditional school settings. One program that has made the national media because of its journey to the U.S. Supreme Court is the school voucher program in Cleveland. This program has provided parents with a voucher equal to about half of the state funds available that the parent can spend at any private school of their choice.

This program was being challenged in court because the vouchers can be used at schools affiliated with religious organizations. It doesn't mandate that they be used at religious schools, but the reality is that the schools that are not religious are too expensive for most students to attend, even with the voucher help. In June 2002, the court handed down a decision establishing the constitutionality of the Cleveland program, paving the way for other programs across the country.

Another program that established community (charter) schools redirects the state basic funding amount for a student to the charter school, an Ohio nonprofit corporation. The charter school may also qualify for the building money and any federal grants for students they are serving. They do not receive the local property tax and local income tax dollars, however. This means that they are operating on between 30 and 90 percent of the funds that the public school down the block is receiving to educate the same student.

Of the 611 school districts in Ohio, about 100 are well funded, spending $15,000 to over $20,000 per year per student. You'll find indoor Olympic-sized pools, full sports programs for boys and girls, foreign languages in elementary school, gifted programs, small class sizes, and many other extras that combine to offer a very positive educational environment. Any child who lands in one of these school districts is fortunate. These districts will serve children out of the bell curve much better and have the resources to address many of the social problems creeping into their communities. Most of these districts are located in the suburban areas around the big metropolitan areas: Columbus, Cleveland, Cincinnati, Dayton, Toledo, Youngstown, Akron, and Canton. ECOT has had some, but not many, students enrolled from these districts.

The other 500 are either resource-poor rural districts or large urban districts. Columbus has about $10,000 to spend per student and many areas are only allotted from $6,000 to $9,000. These districts also have less parent involvement, more poverty, and many social challenges to contend with. More problems and less money are a recipe for lower-quality education for the children who live there. These districts also share a lower voter turnout. As the legislature has wrestled with how to fix this funding inequity, the political reality is that the voters in the rich school districts have more clout because they actually vote and contribute to political campaigns.

As this political brawl rages, a stranger walks into town. While the rich districts and the poor districts are battling over money, this stranger claims he can educate their children for less money than even the poorest district spends. It brings back images of the Wild West and a frontier of uncharted possibilities. The dueling districts now have a common enemy—the statewide chartered e-school that is taking their students and shaming school districts into explaining why they need as much money as they claim they do.

This is where the plot gets complicated and you can count on both hands the number of people in the state who truly understand it. I'm not sure I'm one of them. The reason I am still unclear is that the State Department of Education appears to be making up the rules as they go. They have taken their legislative mandate, which you will learn was developed over several years, and expanded their bureaucratic power way past the test of reasonableness, with the apparent purpose to make charter schools roll over and play dead. This behavior, coupled with their long-standing ineptitude at doing their basic job of writing checks, leaves one to wonder whether they truly understand that they are servants of the people. They are there to serve students by serving the school districts and charter schools that they attend. Somewhere along the line, they have misplaced their priorities, contributing to the crisis in education placing all of our children at risk.

ECOT is a public school that provides free education to any student in Ohio who chooses to enroll. Our funds to provide our basic services come from the taxpayers of Ohio. So far, not so complicated. The way school districts are paid for the students they educate is this. During the first full school week in October each year, the schools count noses, literally. If students are physically at school that week, they are counted. That number is multiplied by the state basic funding amount for that district. That is the amount the district will receive for that school year. It is not adjusted for dropouts, move-ins, or truancy rates. It is fixed. If only half of the students actually attend class or if students who are there learn nothing, the amount does not change.

If a charter school opens in that district and draws 10 students away from Elm Street Elementary, the district's payment from the state will be reduced by 10 times the state basic funding amount (approximately $4,800.) The school district will keep their property tax revenues to be spread out across fewer students, so the per-student spending actually goes up in many districts when charter schools are established. Some districts have claimed that the formula for standardizing the cost of doing business actually results in their district contributing a portion of their property tax revenues to the charter school.

But this is not a zero sum game, as it might appear. The state's formulas leave out a very big variable. Take the situation of a student who was not on the roles at a local school district when he or she enrolled at a charter school. Maybe the student had been home-schooled or had dropped out two years earlier. Or maybe the student had just moved to the area. When the district gets their regular payment from the state, these children will be "deducted" from the payment, even though they were never included in the original calculation. Logic would say that they should be added in before they are subtracted out, but they are not. So the school district is losing funding for a child they didn't even know existed 24 hours before they got the bill. I can imagine that this is like a man being served with a child support order for the child of a woman he doesn't even remember meeting. It has to be a mistake.

Another purely bureaucratic process that contributed to the bad dream experienced by each superintendent in the state at the beginning of our first year was that the State Department of Education required that we estimate our enrollment two months before we opened our doors. We used a statistical model to project where we thought our students would come from. It turned out that we were amazingly accurate on a county-by-county analysis, but not as accurate when you look at the school district-by-school district count. We knew that our initial payments from the state would be based on this estimate.

What we didn't know was that they would rely on it to bill each district for the number of students we had estimated. This would be like opening a pizza parlor and estimating your market at 100 deliveries within a three-mile radius for next Friday night. When Friday night rolls around, you instruct your drivers to just show up at 100 houses randomly and demand payment for the pizza they ordered. You may have hit the total number ordered right on the head and be accurate about the territory, but there is no way you can guess the exact houses. And the people living in those houses that you randomly selected are going to be outraged. Especially the ones on a very tight budget unable to buy basic groceries, let alone pizza.

The Big Eight school districts had seen charter schools open in their districts the year before we started, so they knew what that line item deduction on their state payment was paying for. And if you have 50,000 students and charter schools take 300 of them, you are not terribly disabled by the shortage of 1.5 million dollars out of your $500 million budget. But if you are running a district with 1,500 students and 10 students leave, that $48,000 that goes with them may mean you have to fire a friend of yours. And if those 10 students were just a figment of someone's imagination, you are ready to do battle. I know I would be.

With one mailing, the State Department of Education woke up the other 603 superintendents in Ohio to the reality of charter schools. None had been opened in those districts and therefore none had ever been asked to "pay" for students to attend them. By opening a statewide school that drew students from potentially every district, we gave them an opportunity for a very quick education. It was a course they had not registered for.

The old adage, "Follow the Money," is applicable to the analysis of the problems with public education. The current system of distributing funds has so many flaws that any minor change in the process sends chills up the spines of 611 superintendents simultaneously. To understand the incredible political backlash we have endured begins with understanding the money trail. And since no one really does understand it, we leave ourselves open to mass confusion and hysteria.

The difference between a school district and a business is that school districts cannot go out of business. If they need more money, they can ask for more taxes. They can be taken over by a city or a state if they find themselves in a financial emergency. But they are simply not allowed to go away. This causes very different fiscal planning processes than what we see occurring in businesses. There is very little emphasis on reducing costs or increasing efficiencies. The establishment's biggest fear is, "They're going to figure out that we don't need this much money." Because their cry for the last 50 years has been, "If you just give us a little more money, then we can do a better job." And we keep giving them more money and we keep giving them more money. Test scores are down. It's almost the reverse. The more money they get, the worse the product is.

The simple fact is that there is enough money to go around to educate every child. It is true that you can find ways to spend over $20,000 to educate a child and provide him or her with a country club atmosphere. It is also true that you can spend less than $5,000 and prepare a child for entry into any college in the country. E-schooling reduces the cost, increases the quality, compounds choices, and scares the apples off the desks of teachers and administrators everywhere. It threatens the infrastructure of the school systems that they have built and defended for decades. If, all of a sudden, we can prove that they are spending much more money than it really takes to teach a child, all their complaints about not having enough money fly right out the window.

Graduate Profile:
QUIANA

Imagine, if you will, a worse way to spend your summer after eighth grade than in the hospital, paralyzed from encephalitis. Quiana can't. It was a nightmare. A very healthy, active, 13-year-old one day, a critically ill child the next. It shattered her world and put the lives of everyone who loved her on hold. Quiana had to relearn every movement. She wouldn't have made it without the help of her family and dozens of caring professionals. They were all convinced that she would walk again. Their love convinced her.

I would certainly understand if Quiana wanted nothing to do with hospitals ever again! On the contrary, however, she dreams of becoming a pediatrician. She can't imagine having a more important job than helping sick children.

When Quiana began ninth grade, on time, her doctors and teachers advised her to wait. But she needed to get back into life and was not going to miss her first day of high school. She took it slowly, though, and didn't participate in many extra activities. Her friends were picking up the pace with the new world of high school, but Quiana needed time to fully recover.

By the beginning of tenth grade, she was good to go! A summer of rest brought back the normal, outgoing, active Quiana. She remembers that it was difficult for her friends to accept her new energy level, which caused conflicts. She lost her motivation for school and began falling behind.

Quiana's parents were concerned and helped her find a newly opened charter school on the other side of Columbus. She was critical of their curriculum, however, because she felt she needed more aggressive courses to prepare her for college. With the social issues resolved, she again excelled at her studies and made up for her blown tenth-grade year.

Quiana found ECOT through a strange sequence of events. Her charter school closed due to mismanagement just at the time she learned that she was one physical education credit short of graduation. She started calling other public and charter schools to see if they could help. When she called us, we were happy to help her graduate on time.

Quiana is attending Columbus State Community College and thinking of transferring to Franklin University, a private four-year college in Columbus where her sister will be starting a Master's program this fall. Quiana knows she will be an "old lady" by the time she finishes all the degrees and residencies required to be a pediatrician. She is not daunted, however, as she also knows that she wouldn't even be a young lady without the efforts of all the doctors who helped her in eighth grade. Quiana wants to be able to offer the same care that she received that disastrous summer to children.

Being so close to death or permanent disability taught Quiana lessons that no school can ever include in a curriculum. Her final physical education class may seem like no big deal, but the mere fact that she was there and able to take it was a very big deal indeed.

8

NOT JUST ANOTHER
PIECE OF PAPER

"The people making the real decisions about
education need to interact with the students more.
Ask us what we need. Things are a lot different
from when they went to school."

Quiana Watson, ECOT Class of '01

When you think about the fact that a charter is really just a piece of paper, it's interesting to add up all the turmoil that charters have created. How could a piece of paper be so controversial? All it does is create a school that will be receiving public tax dollars to educate children.

Probably the key difference between a public school established by a government agency called a school district and a public school established by a charter is control. Community schools, as charter schools are also called, have more similarities to their first cousins, the traditional public schools, than they have differences. But it is the differences that are emphasized in the media and in the minds of many policy makers and stakeholders.

I'd like to emphasize the similarities to help you understand their existence and bring some balance to the public conversation surrounding this solution to our education crisis.

- Charter schools educate children ages 5 through 21.

- Charter schools may not discriminate or have entrance requirements, unless serving an at-risk population (e.g. school dropouts).

- Charter schools cannot charge tuition, except for after-school programs and summer school.

- Charter schools provide instruction based on a curriculum that they develop with assistance and guidelines prepared by the State Department of Education.

- Their students are tested by the State Proficiency Test.

- Their teachers are certificated by the state of Ohio.

- Their teachers receive benefits from the State Teachers Retirement System.

- Other staff receive benefits from the State Employees Retirement System.

Charter schools have regular school years and normal school days. Where the controversy occurs is that charter schools operate a little outside the standard process for establishing a school. A state-chartered (different charter) nonprofit corporation raises and provides the capital for creating the physical structure and the resources needed to build a school. The board of that corporation hires staff and teachers to put the school into action. They receive funding from the state and federal governments, but not from local school districts. They may do fundraising and grant writing to increase revenue and capital. They advertise and compete for students with other traditional public, private, and charter schools.

The basic idea was to give back to local communities some of the control of how their children are educated. Also, the opportunity is intended to spur innovative outside-the-box thinking that might allow the development of new approaches to education. The notion was to release some of the chains that bind traditional schools and see what happens. With the public school industry showing disappointing results, some policy makers believe that the "white paper" approach of starting from scratch with a piece of white paper to design a school would be more successful than trying to unravel the bureaucracies that run the existing system.

The school choice movement finds its roots in the state of Minnesota, a part of the country not known for its reactionary political thought. It was Minnesota that first fashioned a school voucher program that passed constitutional muster. Vouchers were the earliest form of choice offered to parents frustrated with the declining quality of traditional education. The concept was to introduce competition in public education as a way of improving the overall quality of education by allowing the tax dollars dedicated to public education to follow the student. Vouchers have been controversial as parents often choose to use the vouchers to pay the tuition for their children to attend church-affiliated schools. Opponents of vouchers argued that this violates the constitutional mandate of separating church from state and is tantamount to the state endorsing a particular religious affiliation.

Pioneers in Minnesota conceived a new educational choice option that became known as charter schools. The charter school concept is based on the idea that a community or neighborhood knows what is best for its children. If an elected school board represents the public of a given community on educational matters, why can't that same community reclaim that power it has vested in the school board and transfer it to another governing body of its own making? The idea was to inspire parents, teachers, or community activists to conceive their own unique educational models. They could then take that model and "charter" their own school within their community. This is why charter schools are also known as community schools in some states. The school's form is limited only by the imagination of its founders. For example, a group of parents frustrated with an inner-city school plagued by violence or poor results could take matters into their own hands and create a new school in their own neighborhood. Or, a group of public school teachers from a traditional school may have an idea for a school that focuses just on the basics. They are now empowered to charter their own public school with that emphasis.

Charter schools are very much public schools. They receive their funding from the same tax dollars that are directed to traditional public schools. However, similar to the voucher programs, the dollars follow the students from the traditional public school to the charter public school. The other difference is that charter schools are relieved of many of the bureaucratic burdens of traditional schools. This freedom encourages creativity and experimentation. Market forces are introduced. If a new charter school is not working, there is nothing that forces parents to keep their children in the school. Likewise, if a new charter school is successful, the traditional public school will feel the competitive heat and be forced to adapt and change if it is to survive. In the end, the children receive a better education and are free to choose how that education is delivered.

Some states allow for-profit corporations to manage charter schools. This situation always attracts detractors with the idea that someone who intends to make a profit could never have the students' best interest at heart. This couldn't be further from the truth. The profit motive is a self-liquidating system. Rather than the self-preservation motive of nonprofit corporations, the profit motive automatically guides a school to efficiency and effectiveness at the same time. If not, the school loses students and fails. No bureaucracy would be needed to notice that the schools were not performing. Since we are paying the charter schools amounts of money per child that would instantly close the traditional schools, I can't see any danger in adding a motivation to be efficient.

With government-run schools, the normal way to seek suppliers is to ask for bids. Suppliers catch on very quickly that cutting the price is no guarantee that they are getting a loyal customer. They have to bid the following year as well. For-profit corporations may look for low prices, but at the same time want to develop a relationship with their suppliers. They want service after the sale and discounts in the future. Many of the maintenance issues in public schools can be traced to the lack of follow-up service from vendors or to vendors who went out of business trying to compete in a low-bid environment. Astronaut and Ohio Senator John Glenn, a hometown hero, is often asked what it felt like to be launched into space. One of his favorite responses to that question that always gets a laugh is, "How do you think you'd feel on top of 2 million parts built by the lowest bidder on the government contract?" Shouldn't we ask ourselves why we are launching our kids into life with the lowest-bid facilities, equipment, and services that our school districts can find?

As with any political change that requires the input of diverse and opposed constituencies, things will never be simple. Some states have had a longer history with this approach to education, notably Arizona, Michigan, California, New Jersey, Texas, Colorado, and Florida. Ohio legislators tried the front-door approach in the mid 1990s by introducing legislation that would establish charter schools in Ohio. The bill passed in one house and failed in the other.

In 1997, the supporters tried another approach. Instead of a stand-alone bill, an amendment was tacked onto the annual budget bill. It passed with the budget bill. This method of establishing law has both pluses and minuses. When a bill is crafted as a stand-alone bill, the legislative service commission will research all the aspects and impacts of the proposed law, alert lawmakers to possible problems and omissions, and then draft a comprehensive bill. A budget amendment, on the other hand, is not generally researched as thoroughly and not debated as heavily. For innovative concepts where many of the potential problems are not yet known, this is an easier way to initiate the change. Follow-up legislation is then used to iron out the issues that couldn't have been foreseen.

This first amendment provided for the Lucas County Education Service Center to conduct a five-year pilot program. This agency had existed to provide innovative educational services to school districts in the Toledo area. Its director, Tom Baker, had been a strong supporter of charter schools and helped to bring the concept to legislators in Ohio.

The program was quickly extended to allow the Big Eight urban school districts the ability to charter schools, even though none of them embraced the idea. By 1999, Lucas County's pilot program was made permanent and the initiative was expanded to allow new charter schools in any of the state's largest 21 urban school districts and any other district rated as being in "academic emergency" by the state's district report card system.

By this time there were 15 charter schools in operation in these school districts serving about 2,200 students. During the 1999–2000 school year, 46 schools enrolled over 9,000 students. The 2000–2001 year saw 68 schools serve 16,000 students. That was also the first year when statewide schools were allowed to form, even though the notion of electronic schools was nowhere in the discussion when the laws were passed.

As the momentum grew, the opposition was mounting. A lawsuit was filed challenging the creation of charter schools by a coalition of educational interest groups. The outcome of that case is yet to be determined, but it has kept alive the debate over the legitimacy of charter schools and the media's attention to their existence.

Even though there are 92 community schools in Ohio serving 23,280 students, 110 have received charters. Twenty percent are no longer in business. What this might suggest is that it is easy to get a charter in Ohio, but not as easy to keep one. Our experience might shed some light on the difficulties faced by community schools although other schools have had difficulties that even we didn't have.

The big issue seems to be under-capitalization. Capital is the resource that businesses use along with labor to generate a product. It is usually gathered in the form of long-term debt or equity ownership investments in a for-profit business. Charter schools are prevented by the statute from entering into long-term debt over one year. They are nonprofit corporations and, therefore, can't sell stock. Since capital is the foundation of any successful business, the school will be shaky from the start without a firm financial footing. It will be vulnerable to any subtle changes in its business plan and will certainly not be able to withstand any unexpected problems. Capital is what gives a business the flexibility to get through their start-up period and settle into a sustainable position.

Traditional schools have the power to go to the voters for bond issues when they need capital investment in their facilities. This long-term debt allows them to spend more than they could levy in one tax year to build the infrastructure that is needed for a stable school. One wonders how a state government could hang out a sign that says, "Come build a school in our state" but prevent the builder from using a foundation. It would never pass inspection by even the most nearsighted building inspector. Any financial inspector will quickly determine that this is where most charter schools will fail as well.

By doing this, the people who have been attracted to seek charters have either been very naïve or very clever or just very determined. Or all three. The numerous news stories that have pointed out financial "mismanagement" at the schools that failed have neglected to point out this tremendous handicap. They will only say that they were losing money, or not paying their teachers, or not exercising good management practices.

I would agree. None of the charter schools in Ohio are exercising good management practices. They are prohibited from doing so by state law. In order to follow the law, the school must somehow fold all of their start-up costs into their revenue from their first year in operation or "float" them in their cash-flow using trade credit and other short-term obligations. It's possible, as we have shown, to do it this way, but it would never show up in a graduate business school textbook under the heading of good fiscal management practices.

The next issue faced by community schools is that they operate on between 30 and 90 percent of the revenues received to educate the same child in a traditional public school. This again is where the naiveté, cleverness, and determination come into play. Certainly a lot of community schools have been able to show that a school can be run for much less than the traditional public schools receive. The external controls on quality come from both the oversight from their chartering authority and their customers, the students and parents. If they cut corners too much, they run the risk of noncompliance with state and federal regulations or of losing students who are not satisfied.

Additional pressure is put on these schools in the form of additional record keeping and audit functions. The intent of the legislature appeared to be to allow creative, dedicated people into the arena of education without the same constraints they found in traditional school systems. What has happened seems to be the exact opposite. Because they were given very little direction by the laws, the bureaucracies charged with supervising education have written a whole new set of rules and regulations. The amount of thought that has gone into these rules is not much more than went into the original laws. This has caused confusion and additional expense for the community schools to try to understand and keep up with continually changing regulations.

There is currently a stand-alone charter school bill that hopes to clarify many of the issues that are causing administrative nightmares for charter schools in Ohio. A new association of charter schools in Ohio hopes to continue to build a voice that will help charter schools succeed. The energy level of this talented group of entrepreneurial educators will not last forever if the rules continue to change. We may lose more schools for no good reason other than overregulation, something the entire notion of charter schools was intended to avoid.

Graduate Profile:
KARITA

Life in a little town in Ohio isn't much different from life in any little town in America. You know just about everybody and they know you. St. Mary's, in western Ohio, is about as small as a town can be and still have a high school. Karita went to Memorial High because the Catholic high school was a fair drive across the county and her mother couldn't juggle the drive while caring for Karita's younger sister, who is disabled.

After eight years at the Catholic K–8 school in town, Karita was used to clear rules and swift enforcement. She was shocked, to say the least, when she arrived at Memorial in ninth grade to find people with dyed green heads and body piercings. Their language was just a bit different as well. Words that were never tolerated in middle school were heard constantly ringing throughout the halls. Kids would smoke cigarettes and chew snuff in the basement of the school. Fights were common. Karita learned that skipping school was barely noticed and not punished.

She also noticed that the pace of education was much slower. She missed an environment where she could question and discover things on her own. It seemed that at this school they just wanted her to memorize facts and spit them back out. Karita began skipping school at least once a week and remembers sharing homework with a friend by changing the name at the top of the paper and turning it in again.

The teacher never caught her.

Then, in eleventh grade, the school got a new principal, a well-liked member of the community with a background in coaching. The environment changed overnight. Karita felt discriminated against because the new principal only liked the kids who played sports. During one visit to his office, she remembers that he told her he wanted her to fear him.

Karita left and was able to attend a neighboring school district by moving in with her grandfather. That school was an opportunity for a fresh start. As a senior, she wanted to attend the vocational school to study graphic design. However, she needed to transfer back to Memorial to do this. That lasted about one week before Karita was begging her mother to get her out of there.

Karita's mother went to the library to research homeschooling regulations. The librarian mentioned that a family member of hers was attending ECOT and that they should check it out. Karita was willing to try anything that would get her out of going to Memorial.

At first, she used her own computer. As she was spending most days babysitting for her nephew, she would print out her work and take it with her. Her boyfriend (now husband) helped her with the difficult lessons. Karita found the work much harder than the assignments at public school. It reminded her more of the level of difficulty at her Catholic K–8 school.

She found that the poor study habits she had developed in high school followed her to ECOT. She would often procrastinate, waiting until the last minute to turn in assignments. She remembers having to pull a true all-nighter to finish a paper for an English class. She found that it was easy to fill her days with activities that were more interesting than school-work. The only motivation she had to complete her work was the thought that she would have to go back to her high school if she got kicked out of ECOT.

Karita was not going to be one of the kids in her town who didn't finish high school. She said it seemed as if only half of the 80 or 90 kids in her freshman class made it to graduation. The others either got pregnant, went to jail, or dropped out because of drug use. Many who graduated went on to college while others could barely read.

Karita enrolled at a business college in Fort Wayne, Indiana, and found the curriculum much too basic. She was also appalled at the high school behavior of the students. The classes were unruly and the students didn't take anything seriously. She knows that she had been guilty of the same attitude during high school, but it was time to get serious about her education and career choices.

Karita withdrew to work full time and get ahead financially before she enrolls in a four-year college next fall. She is undecided about a major at this point but very decided about her personal responsibility for her future. She is not about to skip life the way she skipped classes.

9

ALL POLITICS IS LOCAL

"At my old school I could miss class and not miss much."

Karita McDermitt, ECOT Class of '01

If politics is the art of governing, lobbyists are the paint suppliers. They help to bring variety to the palette of the lawmakers and policy makers. As a lobbyist in the '80s, I was a link between business and government, trying in my own way to help both become successful and efficient.

We don't often think of schools as government agencies. Their assets are owned by the government; their employees carry government pensions; and they must use political maneuvering to impact change and carry out their agendas. Sounds like a government agency to me.

As a charter school, ECOT is a hybrid government agency and business. We are about 90 percent government. The piece that makes us a business is that we can go out of business. As a result, we must use business strategies to develop our mission and ensure our future. One of those business strategies is to try to work efficiently with the government that we are a part of. But what if that government is not sympathetic to our mission and our existence? Because what we do may appear threatening to entrenched interest groups or government bureaucrats, we sometimes find ourselves in the position of having to defend our very existence. This singular activity drains our resources in the form of legal fees and staff time in order to address the latest attack from the government or educational establishment.

The exciting part about this is that someday when the opposition calms down, all those resources will be available to spend on the kids. It is amazing to me that the government pays us money to educate kids and then sometimes puts all its weight behind making sure we have to divert a chunk of that money to argue with them. I am not advocating that we should not be accountable, but I am asking that we be told what we are accountable for.

But, those of us who have the vision and passion for e-schooling see well beyond the shortsighted, current budget cycle-minded bureaucrats who have been charged with supervising our activity. I know they don't yet see what we see and it is our job to be patient while they find their glasses. I also know that it is their nature to protect the status quo, whatever it may be. About the time they stop fighting us at every turn, e-schooling will then be an idea that they started, funded, and supported. In the meantime, there are battles to win and students to teach.

Just like most wars throughout history, this one has several fronts. Those defending the fronts would like them to stay put just where they are. But our fronts are not geographic—they are financial. Following the money from the taxpayers to the school districts does not uncover the entire picture. Those school districts actually do spend that money. And just about every direction where the money goes will uncover another front that we have to battle.

At a dinner with the vice president of a major textbook publishing company, I was told that I would put them out of business in 10 years. My response was that if they went away, who would write our curriculum? Just because we didn't want their material on paper did not mean that students wouldn't be clamoring for the latest, most accurate information to study. And it didn't mean that their profit margin should suffer. It might mean that demand for their services would increase as the production and delivery cycles would shrink and curricula could be updated more frequently. It also meant that more exact and targeted curricula would be requested that previously wouldn't have made it out of the proposal stage as their markets were too small. I'm sure there will be publishing houses that hold onto the old models and put themselves out of business. That will be their choice. I will be there ready and willing to help them become even more profitable under the new paradigm.

Most generals in these battles have not been as willing as that executive to come to the table. They have established a mindset that holding their ground and rallying their troops is the best long-term strategy. The teachers' unions come to mind. I mean, of course, the unions and not the dedicated individuals who are actually standing in classrooms teaching students every day. These unions, on the other hand, have evolved into organizations that do not always have the teachers' primary interests at heart. The main interest should be how teachers can be better equipped to teach kids. Instead, the unions today have limited their focus, nearly to the exclusion of everything else, to retain power and control issues. They have been able to negotiate strong contracts with public school districts and know that their strength is not in the institutions outside of those governmental employers. They also have held onto the "we know best" philosophy for quite some time, seeing parents as more of a distraction than an asset to the education process. As parents have demanded choice in education for their children, unions, not teachers, are the first to feel threatened.

Teachers' unions do not yet see my long-term view about the value of e-schooling to the overall quality of education in the country. The mere notion that teachers can return to being teachers and give up their roles as social workers, police officers, and hall monitors should excite them all summer long, but they don't see it yet. Focusing on students, curriculum, and where the two meet to create positive learning experiences is where I see the role of teachers. Giving them e-learning tools to do this creatively, efficiently, and powerfully is my goal. Teachers should be thrilled and will be as they see how it plays out in their ability to impact the lives of children. If their unions choose to live in the old system, they may find themselves coping with dwindling membership and fighting lost causes. That is their choice. We don't need the teachers' unions. Only the teachers' unions need the teachers' unions. It is projected that the market for qualified teachers will be so tight in the future that teachers' salaries will automatically rise and other work conditions will step up automatically to attract these professionals.

There is another group I'm not sure I can help: the people who make and drive the buses. If we reduce the number of students who need to be transported great distances to school, we reduce the number of buses we need. Buses were a 20th-century logistics solution to the fact that the child and the education were in different places. In the 21st century, we can take the education to the child, eliminating the need to take the child to the education. Hence, we will need fewer buses. We don't need buggy whips any more either and those manufacturers went on to produce new products that were in demand at the time. Their employees went to work for Ford. This is the strength of the greatest economy to ever exist. I don't feel the need to apologize, only the need to spread the word that school bus driving may no longer be a growth industry.

Builders are also threatened, but not quite as organized to rally against this threat as some other groups. We already have a dwindling need for new school buildings as our population has stabilized. Older buildings need to be rehabilitated or replaced, however. If more students stay home to go to school, with or without e-schooling, we will be building and rebuilding fewer schools in the future. I do believe that those dollars and real estate previously dedicated to schools will be redirected to community centers, sports facilities, and other kid-centered buildings. Someone will have to build and rebuild them. The construction industry is much more vulnerable to the winds of the economy and market fluctuations compared to teacher's unions.

A group that surprised me in their opposition to ECOT, until I understood that they usually parrot positions taken by the unions, was the PTA. Parent Teacher Associations do a tremendous amount of good, mainly in finding ways to get parents back in the schools, involved and interested. They have very little actual power in the political landscape other than mobilizing their members to support local tax issues. They have filed a lawsuit against charter schools, claiming they are unconstitutional as a separate school district. They also tend to preach to the choir. The parents who become active are those who like the school they have chosen for their children and they want to see it remain strong. The parents who would rather yank their children out, but have no choice, tend not to invest energy volunteering for the PTA. Many PTAs around the country were the first to raise funds to buy technology for their schools. As soon as they understand the major implications for expanded educational opportunities for their children, they will embrace e-schooling as the next step in technology.

All other vendors, from the suppliers of cafeteria food to audio-visual manufacturers, can find reasons to be threatened by the concept of e-schooling. I don't know where the final balance will land, but much of e-schooling will still happen in traditional buildings where children gather. Some will happen in homeschooling environments and some in new untraditional settings, like juvenile detention centers. Businesses that service school systems will still have the same number of customers; their customers just may be organized differently and located in new places. Some vendors will lose market share and some will gain. Staying ahead of the market and listening to their customers will keep them competitive and profitable. Diversifying now into areas of demand that new school models create will ensure their ongoing success.

These political players, the suppliers of the business of education, will lobby, negotiate, and position themselves to protect their own self-interest, as they should. Some will be brave enough to jump the fence into the new century and look for ways to support the new schools and their mission. If we believe that the cost of this new system of education will be less than the old system, then someone will not be getting the business anymore. Pretty obvious. As far as personnel changes, the teachers will comprise a higher percentage of the workforce than they do now, with administrators and support personnel reducing their numbers. Those workers will find positions in the agencies next door that specialize in the other needs of children not specifically identified as education.

The main source of opposition through this revolution will be school superintendents. If the schools behaved as a business, superintendents would be the CEOs. If they were presented with a way to serve the same number of customers at a higher level of quality for half the money, they would be the first to sign up. But they are not business people; they are government employees who have been trained to manage budgets and beg for more. As soon as it appears that they might get less, they have automatic reactions. This is testimony to their professionalism. They are doing the job their school boards hired them to do: maximize the amount of money coming into their school district. If they spend more than the next district, property values will increase and the school board members will be up for reelection.

Underneath this bureaucratic exterior, I do believe that school superintendents care about children, although their day-to-day role is so removed from the child's experience that they can't be everywhere at once. While they have been vocal in their opposition to our school, their principals have been sending us students. In one budget cycle, they haven't been given a lot of flexibility to make this transition work. Over time, they will see the reduced cost to them of trying to serve students they do not have the size or the specialized programs to handle. They will be clamoring for more e-schooling in their community, not less. They will invite it into their school buildings and happily write the check.

In 1999, Apple Computer joined with the Columbus Public Schools for a pilot project at West High School, the first of its kind in the nation. It attracted national attention, not only for its innovation but also for its results. The ACOT project picked 100 students randomly to ensure the statistical validity of the results. The students involved in this project all graduated and 75 percent went on to college, statistics that this high school had not seen in its 100-year history. The results were so shocking that those involved came to doubt the underlying system and questioned the established bureaucracy. But with as great a trial and as innovative a company as Apple behind it, the Columbus Public School District could not keep it going. Governments are totally out of their element when they carry the ball of innovation. They are followers, not leaders.

We are also up against the very basic human reaction to someone coming in and making us look bad. It is a unique individual who can look at someone else's effort to help them fix a serious problem and not feel just a little embarrassed that they needed the help in the first place. Consultants around the world find this dilemma every day. A company has a problem that the employees would rather live with than shake up the system. So the CEO brings in the "highly paid consultants" and gets the job done. The employees will rarely hug the consultants on the way out the door for solving this nagging problem. Instead, they will criticize the solution, the cost, the new situation they have to get used to, and the consultant for doing something that was "obvious."

The only difference between ECOT and the highly paid consultants is that we are not highly paid. We have been invited in as a charter school to fix the eroding quality of public education. The employees in the current system would rather live with the problem than shake up the system enough to fix it. Their first strategy is to try to put us out of business by being the most difficult system to work with that one could imagine. Their next strategy was to play with our payments. Withholding money, changing the formulas by which we are paid and making us jump through new hoops each month to qualify for the payments that we have earned are effective strategies if you are working with other bureaucrats. However, when you are working with entrepreneurs, those strategies just tend to strengthen the resolve that there is a serious problem to be fixed. Why else would an agency need to resort to such tactics?

This brings us back to the art of government: politics. Former Speaker of the House Tip O'Neill once said: "All politics is local." A school district is about as local as you can get when you look at governmental subdivisions. The policy decisions made by the state are made by the state legislators, who represent rather small geographic/population areas. This is where the decisions will be made. The parents, aka the voters, in these school districts and the legislative districts will communicate with their votes, their contributions, and their letters. They will let the government agencies know that they are failing and demand that new and innovative solutions be put on the table.

ECOT is the largest school in the state of Ohio. We are serving students that other schools have shunned. We are doing it for less money than the poorest district in the state. We are the largest charter school in the country. Yet, the Superintendent of Public Instruction for the state of Ohio has never visited ECOT. Not once has this most senior administrator for public education in this state ever so much as called us to objectively see firsthand what we are doing. We would welcome a discussion of our shared vision of quality education for all children. Instead, our only communications to date have been by way of a request for a special audit, innumerable memoranda and correspondence questioning our funding, and actual interception of our funding.

Of course, ECOT is not alone. Everywhere in the nation that new and innovative alternatives to conventional educational delivery systems, such as e-schooling, have been presented, the establishment reacts violently. However, it is changing. Maybe too slowly for some, but time is on our side. The entrenched bureaucracies who fight us today will have no choice but to join us tomorrow. The proof will be in our success. And with success comes recognition. Recognition that something works is more powerful than any teachers' union or government bureaucracy. We are driven by the fact that parents care about their kids. In the end, at the risk of sounding trite, we are ultimately in control of our own destiny.

Graduate Profile:
JESSY

Jessy loves computers. Her mom got a computer a couple of years ago but locked it in her bedroom, off limits to the kids, when she found Jessy's brother cruising chat rooms that were not healthy. Jessy was already hooked. She enjoys finding new Web sites and learning new programs. She is currently learning to use her scanner to create a CD of family pictures so that everyone in her family can have copies of pictures from their childhood.

Jessy's path to ECOT was not a pleasant one. She was delighted to find us but wishes it could have been under less stressful circumstances. School started out fairly normally for her as a student in Zanesville, Ohio, a county seat about 75 miles east of Columbus. She attended both public and Christian elementary schools, saying the only differences between the two were the uniforms and the science curriculum. She liked both schools but remembers wishing they could make up their minds about how the world got started. In third and fourth grades, her school had a curriculum called Paces that allowed students to work at their own level in each subject. Jessy really liked that concept.

Public middle school started out rough. By December of seventh grade, Jessy had gotten into four fights. Her mother pulled her out and enrolled her at a Christian middle school. Things calmed down for her and, by ninth grade, Jessy's mother felt she should return to public school. Zanesville High was a good environment for Jessy. She particularly liked the fact that blacks and whites got along well and that, as a white, she could have black friends.

When Jessy was in tenth grade, her mother moved to Newark, a rival of Zanesville, in the next county over. Jessy wasn't used to the racial tension she found there and it bothered her. She didn't like being there and kept to herself. She began to smoke cigarettes and had to sneak around to feed her habit during the school day. She would leave the school grounds at lunch, which was against the rules, to have a cigarette.

One day the truancy officer caught Jessy off campus and disciplined her with a detention. In the parking lot, on her way to the detention, the principal stopped Jessy and smelled cigarettes on her. She insisted on searching Jessy's car. Jessy jerked her hand back as the principal was reaching for the car keys. Jessy hit the principal in the face with her keys and was charged with assault. She was convicted and given a juvenile sentence, which ended with a period of "in school suspension" where she was not allowed to attend classes but had to sit in a room inside the school building during school hours. Jessy withdrew from school rather than waste her time in this room. A guidance counselor suggested ECOT.

Jessy immediately went to our Web site and then attended the orientation in Columbus with her mother and brother. Jessy and her brother both signed up. Jessy worked full time during the day while her brother used the computer. Then Jessy used the computer in the evenings into the early morning hours. She found her schoolwork difficult and didn't have a lot of contact with her teachers. Although she found the work interesting and liked working on a computer, she didn't have anyone to help her as no one in her family had graduated from high school.

Jessy's full-time job allowed her to save a good deal of money. She was able to buy her own car and her own computer. She is also paying her own tuition to attend college online, studying Web design with Thomson Education Direct. She is enrolled in a two-year Associate's degree program that she will complete in one year. Then she intends to complete an Associate's degree in business administration. Jessy is very proud to say that she will have two degrees by age 20.

10

DIVIDED DIGITALLY

"Schools should concentrate on teaching.
What we do before and after school
is not their concern."

Jessica Ricciardo, ECOT Class of '01

Whenever you are first at something, excitement and danger come in the form of not knowing what is ahead. Each morning throughout the last three years, I have woken up wondering what the day will bring and what battles I will need to suit up for. As you look back through the history of business, it is not always the first company in the game that builds up enough to become the biggest and the best. One reason is that all the resources were likely spent blazing trails. Sometimes the trails lead nowhere. But the trails that open up opportunities are there for companies that come behind, following the blaze marks.

One of the more interesting political battles we are waging may turn out to be one of those trails that leads nowhere, or it may change the course of history in the pursuit to bridge the digital divide. The digital divide is the nickname given to the difference in opportunity for those individuals who have access to computers and the Internet and those who don't. At this time, it is estimated that fewer than 5 percent of the people on the planet have the opportunity to connect to the Internet. While we think of the Internet as allowing us to talk to people everywhere—that is potentially true— not everyone is yet connected.

As people in the United States often carry their concerns to our borders and no further, the term digital divide is more often used to describe the inconsistent computer access and computer literacy within the United States. This inequality is measured in socio-economic terms, education levels, racial/ethnic terms, geographic terms, age, and probably some others I'm not aware of. We can say that people are more likely to be connected to the Internet if they are high-income earners, well educated, white, live in a big city, and are young adults. These people, of course, are the citizens who already have many advantages and will use the Internet to further advantage. People who are low-income earners, less educated, non-white, live in rural areas, and are older could also use the Internet to their advantage but often don't have access or the skills and confidence to try.

When we started ECOT, we saw the value of bringing computers to children for the purpose of delivering education. We did not immediately know that our efforts would be a big step in helping to bridge the digital divide. At least half of the households where we have installed computers did not have a computer before their children enrolled at ECOT. Many people in government and policy-making positions find it hard to imagine that there are families who still don't own a computer. They are so connected to computers at work and at home that it is easy to forget others are not yet living in the same world.

One of the earlier decisions we had to make was how to connect the students with the school. We knew each student would need a dedicated local phone line. The question was whose name would it be in and who would pay for it. First, we knew that we couldn't charge the families for the phone because that would be seen as a regular, ongoing payment that would translate as tuition in the eyes of the state—a no-no for charter schools. We were also pretty sure that it would be problematic if we asked the family to purchase the phone service and then we would reimburse them for the cost. We couldn't be sure they would use the money to pay the phone bill.

We also learned that if the family had two phone lines in their name, the line would not qualify for federal e-rate funds. This is the political battle that brought us right to the front of the war to fix the digital divide. The Federal Communications Commission (FCC) has a division called the Carrier Bureau, as in telephone carriers. This bureau collects money from everyone who has a phone and deposits this money into a superfund for the sole purpose of helping schools extend technology and telecommunications to disadvantaged students. To determine eligibility, the Carrier Bureau looks at both the student and the school district. They are especially interested in bringing technology to poor rural school districts. The concept is to reduce the cost of telephone service so that those districts can provide better technology for students.

Let's add it up. ECOT enrolls students from poor rural districts. ECOT enrolls students who are disadvantaged on many levels. ECOT provides technology and connectivity to those students. ECOT is paying for the ongoing phone service to provide that connectivity. We comply with every aspect of the law, in practice.

As with many battles we have fought, our concept caught policy makers off guard. It was the same with e-rate. We took the idea and really stretched it. During three trips to Washington, we met with the administrators of the fund. They approved of the idea and we got a 20-minute audience with the FCC, a 20-minute meeting that lasted three hours. By the time we were through with our presentation, they couldn't believe the exciting power of e-schooling to help bridge the digital divide.

About a year later, the meeting took a different turn. We were told that the FCC had 2 billion dollars to spend on the rate tax. Requests from traditional schools at the time totaled about 7 billion. They calculated that ECOT alone could require them to pay 30 billion. The policy problem they had was that if they opened up the fund to e-schools, there would not be enough money in Washington to pay for it.

Now we're fighting the policy problem. Do we comply? Sure. Do we look the part? Yes. Do we have an educational purpose? Yes. Do we own the phone lines? Yes. Are our systems secure? Yes. Are we going to get the money? No. In other words, the battle is not over. We're lining up our Congressmen and Senators and people to help fight that battle in Washington. Being first in Ohio and the first in the country, the problem we have is that we're also the first to change federal regulation. That's not a cheap way to do business.

We have a very difficult task of balancing whether or not we have the resources to fight. If we were to fight and win, we set the stage for every school coming behind us to have it easier. Our decision is to try and fight if we can. This is one of the roles of being a pioneer. We have to follow the money to see where our idea might survive, even if the federal government says we don't have enough money. And yet, subsequent to our trip a week later, an article appeared in the *Washington Post* about how great e-rate was for bridging the digital divide and helping students in rural communities. At the same time, the FCC was denying us.

The speed at which technology is changing may make programs like e-rate unnecessary within a few years. As bandwidth becomes cheaper and faster and as more consumers demand the services, we may have a totally new set of problems—but access won't be one of them. I see this divide as temporary, just as most revolutionary changes in our lives turned out to be. Cars, electricity, television, telephones, and now computers started out as playthings for the rich and eventually filtered down to the majority of the population. You might be shocked to learn, however, that 2 percent of our students did not have local phone service before attending ECOT.

When we think about the applications of the Internet, there isn't one that is more critical to the success of our society than education. Once the access problem is solved, the other aspect of the digital divide that is critical is competence. If you've seen a mature adult install a computer and develop comfort with it in less than a couple of years, I'd be surprised. Computers are not intuitive machines, ready to use without a period of acclimatization and training. But watch a 10-year-old who has been poking at keyboards since she was two: She is fearless and intuitively understands how to navigate, solve problems, and use different software. It's like riding a bike. Once children know how to ride the Internet, they know. If they start early, they'll always know and never be timid.

One area where this age-related difference has become obvious is with our own teaching staff. When they come to work with us, many are not fully trained in computer usage. We have a complete training program that brings them up to the level of competence and then provides them with ongoing support and training as new applications are developed. Very few of our teachers are young enough to have grown up with computers. They had to add computer skills after their brains were hardwired to learn using other mechanisms. It seems similar to phenomena documented about people who are bilingual early in life having an easier time learning additional languages. Those who learn at least some computer applications early in life seem to adopt other applications quickly.

The extension of this theory would be that children who start out learning through computers will be comfortable with that medium throughout their lives. The question is whether the converse is true. Will they be uncomfortable learning in a lecture setting? The ultimate learning environment will combine a multitude of instructional technologies and strategies so that we don't inadvertently create a new divide.

Enough research has been carried out to document different learning styles and the curricula developers have incorporated strategies conducive to the different styles into K–12 curricula. They are now taking this approach into e-learning curricula. Obviously, computers work well for visual learners. By adding voice and other sound, we can accommodate the listening learners. Interactive programming provides tremendous opportunities for the kinesthetic learners.

I envision our model helping to break through the current mindset of what computer education looks like and opening up more possibilities than anyone has contemplated. For example, a student's curriculum could be accessed as we now access our money through ATM machines. Anywhere a student goes, he could gain access to his education with a password. Obviously he could access it at school and at home, but at other settings as well. Companies could expand daycare facilities to accommodate school-age children during their parents' work hours and their education could go with them into that facility.

The world will demand lifelong learning from its productive workers. Much of that learning will be electronic and delivered at the time and place that workers can access it. Education will become self-directed and self-paced. Students who grow up with at least a portion of their curriculum delivered electronically will be ready to self-manage their adult learning requirements. This ability will also divide those who are ready to succeed in the workforce from those who are not.

It is important to bridge the digital divide as soon as we can. I applaud the current government initiatives to accelerate the process. I believe, however, that the market and the work of entrepreneurs will have a greater impact than the government. We know the demand is there and we will continue to look for ways to service it, as the bureaucrats debate how to distribute limited resources.

Graduate Profile:
ELIZABETH

When Elizabeth didn't want to go to her high school because of conflicts with some of the students and because some classes didn't interest her, her parents did not have many choices. Since her father was the city manager of the suburb of Cincinnati where they lived, they were required to live within the city limits. It was a very small school system with no magnet schools.

Elizabeth's parents weren't initially sold on the idea of ECOT. After attending an orientation session in Cincinnati, they were convinced that Elizabeth would be happier finishing her education at home. They were very interested in seeing her graduate. If ECOT could help her reduce her stress and continue her education, they were all for it.

Elizabeth liked her classes at ECOT. Her favorites were English, Art, and Economics. She felt all her teachers were dedicated and truly interested in giving her a good experience. They kept her interested in the subjects she was studying and she didn't get bored as she had with lectures at her former high school.

It took a while for the phone line to be installed at her home to hook her up with the ECOT server. Finally she was able to connect anytime she needed and found the interaction through the computer very comfortable.

Elizabeth's dream career is working at the world-class Cincinnati Zoo after she majors in zoology or biology in college. While at ECOT, she volunteered as a research assistant on a project designed to determine why a type of small exotic cat was dying prematurely. She was responsible for caring for some domestic cats that were testing vaccinations for the disease that the exotic cats were contracting.

Elizabeth is working for Kroger to build a financial base while she evaluates her college options. Her parents are very proud of her choice to try something brand-new and work hard to reach her goal. They are very sure she will take her next educational step with as much care and courage.

11

LET'S GET CONNECTED

"It wasn't a big deal.

I just stayed home to go to school."

Elizabeth Neal, ECOT Class of '01

The year that the Class of '01 was born, "Terms of Endearment" won the Oscar for Best Picture, Reagan was finishing up his first term as president, and Apple Computers had just come out with its new and improved Apple II+, a revolutionary machine with 32K of memory (expandable to 64K) and an external disk drive that would store a remarkable 256K bytes of information on a removable disk. It was not yet feasible to have two Apples connect to each other for real applications. And the $5,000 price tag ($8,500 in today's dollars) kept them out of most people's homes. Modems could be installed, but it was not yet clear whom you might call with one. And the Internet was just a twinkle in Al Gore's eye.

It really has been that fast. In less than one generation, we have had to adopt an entirely new language to describe (and complain about) this revolution in technology. We have changed our lifestyles almost overnight to welcome and trust this new way of communicating with others, doing business, and running our world. It is now estimated that computers are doubling in speed and capacity while their prices are cut in half about every 18 months. Just about the time we think we've got it, there is something else we need to learn. It has been said that professionals in the computer field have to "start over stupid" every year and relearn their entire job.

I have to admit that I don't just start over stupid each year, I stay stupid all year long! This world is moving so quickly that I feel behind the curve every day. To some people, this would lead to frustration. For me, it has led me through the process of designing this school with the confidence that if a problem isn't solvable today, it very well might be tomorrow. The day that I wake up and believe that I know everything I need to know to make this concept the best it can be is the day it will fail. Excellence in e-schooling is not just a moving target, it's a bullet train. And it's not hanging around the station waiting to see whether we're going to get on.

As I'm writing this today, we are already 18 months past the moment we conceived the first design for the infrastructure of this school. Technological innovations have already changed our platform and more changes are imminent. If we compare ourselves to the brick-and-mortar schools, it would be as if we had built a grass hut, upgraded to a stick structure a few weeks later, then found some lumber a month or two later, and added aluminum siding by the end of the first year. And within the next year, we expect to have a marble palace. Just imagine how busy we could keep the building inspectors!

Cyberspace is a big and scary place to some people. The fact is that it isn't as big and shouldn't be as scary as the first broadcast technologies probably were. Pictures and sounds flying through the air! And landing in a little box in your living room with a piece of wire on the roof to tell those pictures where to land! Does any normal person really understand how that works? Well it has something to do with waves, I'm told. Yet, I expect it to work, get mad when it doesn't, shop for the latest technology, and refuse to get out of my chair to change the channel.

At this moment, most of cyberspace isn't really taking up that much space. It is contained within wires that are very much right here on earth, not somewhere light years away. In fact, I bet you can point to a favorite tree that was trimmed back too far to allow your phone company or cable company to install new wires in order to allow your neighbors a better connection to their cyberworld. Even the places where we store all the information that zips around in cyberspace have gotten much smaller. What used to take a few city blocks to store is now sitting over in the corner of your living room in a small computer unit.

The Internet, as you probably know by now, is just a system that hooks all these wires together so that we can exchange data. When a computer signs on to the Internet, it gets an address that other computers can find like 161.58.10.225. And then we give those addresses cute names like www.eospublishing.com. This is no different than naming 1600 Pennsylvania Avenue as The White House. And when you mail something to The White House, the mail carriers know the address. It is also similar to the system that we take for granted with our phones. Each one has a number that marks its place on the grid.

To understand where ECOT is in cyberspace, we need to explain that there is a big computer, called a server, in Cincinnati, Ohio. This server is always signed on to the Internet and has a specific address. Because up to 3,000 other computers could be requesting data from it at any given moment, the wires that attach to it have great capacity. They are owned by a company called a co-locator that has enough bandwidth to handle all our traffic. We rent the space for our data from Level 3, a co-locator for Internet services. It is up to Level 3, per our agreement, to make sure that our computers are accessible around the clock and that the flow of data in and out is uninterrupted.

So, you see, we do have a structure. Our structure is made out of silicone, plastic, and active electronic impulses. They constantly need upgrading. Whereas a normal school building is replaced every 40 to 50 years, within that same period our school will undergo 30 upgrades at a cost of 100 times the renovation cost of a normal school building. Leasing this space ensures that we are not stuck with old technology at any moment but are always able to take advantage of the latest, fastest, and cheapest means to deliver our education.

If a student lives in Cincinnati, theoretically they could have their modem dial a local phone number that would ring at the Level 3 facility and be tapped into the ECOT server. There would be no additional cost for that connection above the cost of their monthly phone service. As we were planning a system for students through-out the state of Ohio, however, we couldn't use that strategy for everyone. We needed to build a model that would work wherever the student lived and whatever the communications technology in that area would support.

The next strategy that would work for everyone would be to dial a long distance (toll or toll-free) number directly into the ECOT server in Cincinnati. This technology is easily understood and readily available. The only problem is that most long distance providers charge by the minute and we were talking about a situation where 3,000 people would be "on the phone" for up to five or more hours a day! That's almost 20 million minutes of phone time a month. Even "Friends and Family" wouldn't help us with that cost!

That dilemma brought us back to the Internet as a way to connect our students from around the state to the server in Cincinnati. Internet Service Providers (ISPs) are essentially long distance companies, carrying mostly data instead of voice communications at this point. We have contracted with two different ISPs in Ohio to help us cover our bases in case one of them has a failure, either business or technological.

This left us with what is called the "last mile." How do we connect the student with an Internet Service Provider? There were two possibilities: a phone wire or a cable wire. Local phone companies and local cable companies are competing for that last mile service to households in many communities. But only the larger population centers are serviced consistently with cable service like Roadrunner and their monthly rates are much more costly than monthly phone service. All local phone service can carry data at a basic speed and some phone companies are beginning to offer faster modem speed with DSL (Digital Subscriber Line) service.

To our surprise, there are 43 local phone companies in Ohio, with competition just beginning to rev up. Establishing relationships with all these companies and learning the ropes of how to order phone lines and get them installed properly was one of our biggest nightmares. As protected monopolies for years, phone companies have not had to respond to market pressures for efficient customer service. We hope that the opening up of that market will have an impact on this problem. Complaining doesn't seem to work.

So, starting in the student's bedroom, we have:

- The ECOT computer outfitted with a modem and the software to connect with an ISP

- A dedicated local phone line from a local phone company installed in the student's home

- An account with an ISP

- The ISP account that connects them to the server in Cincinnati

In some very remote areas, there is a another provider between the dedicated local phone line and the ISP in the form of a long distance provider because the ISP does not have a local number to call.

With these coordinated technological services—local phone service, long distance service, Internet service, co-locator service, and server maintenance—a student can have school come into his or her bedroom. But, where is the teacher? I have emphasized the miracle of the child being able to be at home but have forgotten to point out that the teacher is also at his or her own home. With the exact same technology, the teacher is connected to the server and, therefore, to all of his or her students, in real time, with no per minute charge. They also use the long distance services to call their students for various purposes.

You might be old enough to remember party lines. If not, let me share a piece of technological nostalgia with you. It used to be that individual phone lines were expensive to have installed. The phone company would give you the option of having a party line, which was essentially an extension of your neighbor's phone. With this type of service, if your neighbor was on the phone, you couldn't be and vice versa. And you could listen to all their conversations if you were devilish. An awful lot of gossip got started this way.

Right now, in Internet service, we are in the "party line phase" of the product development. We all share each other's lines. And with a little bit of insight, you can "eavesdrop" on your neighbor's Internet transmissions. You can actually peek at activity all over the world. And just like the pricing for individual phone lines in the '50s and '60s, pricing for a more private Internet connection is more expensive. This is what we talk about when we use the word secure.

It starts with the ISP giving each student a direct connection to our server in Cincinnati, without allowing them to "call" anyone else that the server doesn't authorize. It also keeps others from calling them. This creates what is called an Intranet. Many large companies develop them for their various locations around the country to keep out competitors and thieves.

With our students, we are not as worried about competitors and thieves as we are about pornographers and pedophiles. It is well known that the Internet has become a breeding ground for inappropriate content for youth. We began our entire planning process with the singular goal of protecting the students. The principal in a brick-and-mortar school knows that her first job, even before educating the students, is to keep everyone safe. Our school is no different. The dangers just took a different form.

The current solution is an Intranet with a secure server. There is no doubt that going to this "private line" from a "party line" is much more expensive. It requires more programming, more equipment, more personnel to monitor it, more policies and procedures and, occasionally, more down time when breaches are suspected. It continues to be our highest priority and one of the areas where the bar is always being raised. In the spring of our second year, a mother phoned into our headquarters and reported that her daughter had run off with a man she met online while using the ECOT computer. This was our worst nightmare. The school was on a complete security stand-down. Within minutes all protocols were tested and the system was put through rigorous testing. This is a much more sophisticated exercise than a fire drill at a brick-and-mortar school. Highly trained technicians are involved at considerable expense.

How did she get to a Web site where this could happen? It turned out that she didn't. It was a hoax to cover up a relationship that she didn't want her mother to discover. But that false alarm did alert us to another breach that we were unaware existed. It was so remote that no one had imagined its possibility. We are learning every day while newer technologies are making it easier to ensure the safety of our children.

Every week in schools across the country, there are security alerts. Searches are conducted, people are interviewed, and students are sent home if conditions are too volatile to ensure their safety. Procedures are then adjusted if additional measures are needed. The only difference between this type of activity and what we do is that most of what we do is invisible to the students. They don't see the police arrive and they don't have to call their parents and go home shaking. It's just a "server day:" a day that you'll hear students compare to the old snow days they wished for at brick-and-mortar schools.

The debate over Internet access for school children and library patrons is raging across the country. The issue of censorship goes to the core of who we are as a nation. The Internet has brought these debates to a new level. Everyone agrees that children should not view pornography. Everyone does not agree on how to protect them from this threat while preserving our constitutional freedoms. While new technologies are developed that provide user-level security, the federal government originally enacted two policies that provided some guidance. The Commission on Online Child Protection Act (COPA) and the Children's Internet Protection Act (CIPA) offered guidelines that were an initial attempt at protecting our children.

This is one of the main reasons why ECOT is providing children with the specially configured hardware, the Internet Service Provider, and the software to attend school at ECOT. We can establish protocols, monitor compliance with those protocols, and assure parents that their children are not attending school in an X-rated movie house. If the family already owns a computer and has an Internet connection, they can choose to allow their child access to ECOT through that connection even though we do not advise this option. In this case, the parents are voluntarily assuming the responsibility for monitoring their child's Internet browsing. Depending upon the age of the child, the location of the computer in the house, and the time of day the child is online, this can be a difficult task. We encourage parents not to assume this risk.

Another risk we have that is similar to a risk in brick-and-mortar schools is vandalism. In a traditional school, the physical facilities can be damaged or stolen. In an electronic school, vandals have to do their damage in a different way. Usually it is through computer hacking, an activity where hackers use Internet connections to hack into our server and destroy or alter data. This possibility is minimized by an extensive security system that includes electronic firewalls, backup protocols, and round-the-clock security personnel trained to notice illegal activity. Our students could, theoretically, be the vandals. As in any other school, they have more opportunity and possibly more motive. It takes a great deal more skill and planning, however, to hack into a monitored secure server than to throw a rock through a window.

I haven't built a brick-and-mortar school, but my guess is that it takes at least a couple of years from the design stage to the day when the first student walks through the door. From the day we engaged the help of Xerox to make this happen to the day our first student completed a lesson online, it was five months. Four months after that, we were serving 2,000 students with varying levels of functionality. Now that the blueprint is done, the next school will take half that time. We have the beginnings of prefab schooling, where the factory can make the next one to specific specifications and ship much faster than building from the ground up.

As you read each of the graduates' profiles, you may notice that some had connectivity problems all year long, some had intermittent problems, and some had no idea what all the fuss was about in the chat rooms. During this ramp-up period, we were dealing with problems at every level of the connectivity channel from the student's bedroom to our server. Whenever a student called to report a problem, we had to evaluate each piece of the channel. Sometimes, a piece of their hardware or software in their computer had malfunctioned. Sometimes it was a problem with their phone company or ISP. Sometimes our server or a curriculum provider experienced a programming problem. And sometimes it was a system-wide server problem. During this experience we realized how critical our relationships are with all of our vendors. None of them abandoned us and all were functioning to our satisfaction by the second semester. We are all in this together: vendors, students and staff. It is truly a team effort to find ways to make the school work.

Graduate Profile:
STEFANIE

Stefanie's mother was proud of her daughter and proud of herself. For six years they had learned together as she homeschooled Stefanie. Together they would look for curriculum and learning opportunities, solve problems, and struggle with new subjects. She had only one regret about pulling Stefanie out of Toledo public schools after fifth grade. She would miss the opportunity to see Stefanie walk across a stage to get her diploma. As her only child, Stefanie was her only chance to enjoy that experience.

Stefanie remembers her years in elementary school as being fun. She made a lot of friends whom she kept in touch with throughout high school. As she progressed, her classes got easier and easier. She was often bored and wanted more time to study the subjects that truly interested her. Stefanie's mother was concerned about her daughter's safety at school. The decision to homeschool was mutual.

Stefanie knew she was keeping up with her former classmates because of the testing and assessments required by the state of Ohio for homeschooled children. She liked the fact that she didn't have "homework" and could finish all her lessons by the time her friends came home from school. She had a lot of time for social activities and sports after school hours. Her favorite activity was rollerblading with her friends.

Stefanie heard about ECOT on the news and attended the orientation. There were so many advantages over homeschooling: less paperwork, less cost, teachers to guide you, computerized curriculum, a diploma from an accredited school, and a graduation ceremony for her mom!

Stefanie knew how much effort went into educating only one student as she had seen the time that her mother had dedicated to her education. She couldn't imagine how much effort it was taking to make a statewide e-school happen. She expected many more problems than she encountered. And she was willing to forgive us for the few that she did experience because she felt we were giving her so much.

Halfway through a semester one of her teachers quit and the new teacher neglected to post any work for Stefanie. She kept looking for her assignments and assumed they would appear when the teacher got organized. What appeared, instead, was a grade of incomplete for the class. Stefanie was understandably irritated because she had been more than willing to do the assignments, had she known what they were. A conference with the teacher straightened out the situation and Stefanie was allowed to finish the work and pass the course.

After six years of homeschooling, having teachers again was a treat. The ability to ask a question and get help right away almost felt like cheating. Stefanie was used to having to research and figure out problems on her own or with her mom. She enjoyed almost all of her teachers and tried to get to know each one.

The independent study aspect of ECOT fit Stefanie like a glove. She liked the time she had to work on assignments. She could finish some quickly and use more time on others. She realizes that for a student to succeed at ECOT they need to be independent learners. They can't be lazy or need someone to push them to do their work. They can't need a lot of attention. Being allowed to work at her own pace kept Stefanie interested in all her subjects.

Stefanie's zest for learning lots in different areas has one drawback: She isn't sure what career she'd like to pursue. She has changed her mind often about which direction to go. At this point, she is working in a day-care center and has narrowed down a career choice to working with children, possibly in the educational field. She was married this winter and will head back to school for her next diploma as soon as she figures out what type of education will help her meet her career goals. And I'm sure her mom will be sitting through at least one more graduation ceremony.

12

THE STRONGEST LINK

"I hope e-schooling becomes a lot more popular because
it's a lot less dangerous than regular schools."

Stefanie Taylor, ECOT Class of '01

For over three decades, parents have been increasingly banned from the education system. Several social issues have impacted this result, including the desegregation of our schools through crosstown busing and the increasingly transient workforce. The current education professionals have inherited a system that was set up to fail. It seemed a decent idea, initially, to garner control from the parents and dictate the child's educational experience. But as schools continued to take on other roles previously carried out by parents, the burden became too great and the parents rebelled. Parents are reacting negatively to schools that are, in essence, telling them how to raise their children.

Instead of being a service to parents, schools have become a controlling force. Unfortunately, over time, parents have allowed this to happen. They have given the responsibility and obligation of educating their children to the school systems: to feed, discipline, educate, socialize, and keep them active after school with extracurricular activities.

For quite some time, the only way to remove your child from this control was to choose a private school. Write a check. Pay a bill. With this simple transaction, a different dynamic takes shape. Parents are more involved. In the Catholic school system, parents are needed to supplement the generally resource-poor workforce. Parents are working bingo, painting classrooms in the summer, and serving on the school board. The natural outcome of this is more parent interaction with the school. And because parents are writing a check, they feel they have a reasonable right to know what is going on and can voice their opinions about their child's education.

The voucher program that is being tested in Cleveland gives parents a similar sense of involvement. Even though the check they spend is the state's money, they are choosing to deliver it to a specific institution. Where do they go? Catholic schools. Is it because Catholic schools have better facilities, better teachers, or better curriculum? Not necessarily. It is because the parents are welcomed as an active, integral part of the education process. This does two things: increases the parent's sense of control and improves the student's educational experience. Most importantly, it changes the culture, which promotes learning.

Public schools have actually turned the corner in the last couple of years and begun to complain that parents don't get more involved in raising their children and supporting the schools. The schools feel they are now carrying too much of the burden. This reminds me of the old saying, "Be careful what you ask for because you might get it!" For as long as I can remember, educators, particularly in elementary schools, have been saying, "Parents, we'll take care of it and we'll do the job." At first it seemed to give them more power to control curriculum, schedules, and their own lives.

When parents become the customers through writing checks, however, schools become customer oriented. They are no longer mini-prisons where we lock up our kids for six hours a day, waiting to see if they learned anything at the end of the day. They are no longer places where we unilaterally trust the professionals to know what is best. Parents become stakeholders, which changes the entire dynamic of the child's experience.

There is no more powerful component to a child's education than having a parent care about his or her performance. By about sixth grade, the student will begin to pretend that it doesn't matter, but child development specialists will tell us that it may be even more important throughout adolescence and the teenage years. The strongest message a child can receive about the value of education results from no one noticing daily mundane things like being able to get away with not doing your homework to more important events like flunking a subject. The ability of a parent and teacher to e-mail back and forth about a child's progress changes the way a child approaches his or her work. It adds accountability to the child's experience and completes the education circuit: parent-child-teacher.

Charter schools everywhere are finding that parents are coming back into that equation stronger than ever. They have wrestled back control from the establishment that previously kept them out. The parents now want back in the school building and the threat is that when parents come back into the school building, they're not going to tolerate what they used to tolerate. Charter schools are inviting parents in for the same reason that Catholic schools do—they need them. Remember that they are providing education for less money than the traditional public school down the block. The parents provide a resource that allows the school to function. If you were to put a dollar amount on the value of the parents' time, you might see that those schools are actually spending much more than the public school with no positive way to involve parents.

Prior to charter schools, many parents chose another option to put themselves back in the equation: homeschooling. Ohio has had a strong homeschooling population for the last 10 years. The early adopters had to pretty much go it on their own. But as more and more families chose this solution, resources became available, curricula were developed, and groups formed to give the children the social interaction they sought. Some of these groups are tremendously active, offering daily opportunities for children to interact and learn. These families were not running away from the notion that a child can learn while around other children. They were, instead, trying to get back some control from the imposing structure that was public education. Many of these families formed their decision on religious grounds, but other have safety or educational reasons for keeping their children out of traditional school buildings.

The outcry against homeschooling usually centers around the lack of socialization opportunities for the child. Another equally passionate cry was how would we know if these children were actually

learning anything, especially since they didn't have the benefit of certificated teachers in front of them. They'd never be accepted into
college. In some minds this was tantamount to child abuse. The parents who chose this route put up with comments and stares that
cause them to continually reaffirm their decision. And make no mistake, they have asked for a difficult job. Teaching is not easy, and
teaching your own child has unique obstacles.

Now that we have 10 years under our belts, what are we seeing?
The homeschooled kids are the stars. Is that because they were smart
to begin with? Some yes, others no. They are sought after by colleges. They are winning the spelling bees, the science fairs, and the
academic team challenges. They are exploring interests, hobbies, and
sports to levels that kids in a school building all day can't experience.
They are working at their own pace, enjoying the learning without
peer pressure and grades. Most important, without question in my
mind, they excel because their parents are there, working with them,
caring about them, and sending them the strongest message possible
that their education is important.

At the inception of ECOT, we thought our market would be
these families. They were already at home, having walked away from
traditional schools. But when they walked away, none of the state or
local funding went with them. Imagine what a family could do with
an extra $5,000 a year to buy resources and experiences to enhance
their child's educational experience. With the charter school law, we
could legitimately funnel that money back into the family through
resources, teachers, and technology. We would eliminate the paperwork hassles that homeschoolers have to endure. We would be able
to provide a true diploma that wasn't questioned by a college or an
employer. The family would have more choices of curriculum at no
cost, supported and monitored by a certificated teacher. This potential market gave us the courage to try the concept.

We thought it would be an easy transition for a student to move from homeschooling to our model. And for those who have done it, it has been. When we thought that 80 percent of our students would come from this population, we had grossly overestimated. Only 10 percent of our students the first year were previously homeschooled. Others were considering the option and ECOT offered them fewer start-up worries and less anxiety about going it alone.

The question, then, was why did we miss the mark on this? What was it that homeschoolers were looking for that we couldn't offer? It seemed to come down to one common denominator: curriculum. As a public school, we cannot offer a faith-based curriculum. Even though we can offer courses that teach the history and culture of religion, we cannot teach or promote a single religion. For many families, this was the key issue that drove them away from traditional schools. We are a public school and that puts us in the same class as the schools they left.

Many curricula exist that serve homeschooling families with the religious content they seek. Very soon, this content will also be offered in an e-schooling environment to those families. The only difference between how it will be delivered and what ECOT offers will be who is paying for it. Now that vouchers are determined to be constitutional when spent on schools owned by religious organizations, that family may be able to use the state's money to pay for that curricula. As a public school, ECOT will not be offering religious curricula, but a family could enroll their child in ECOT and supplement their child's education with religious materials designed for homeschoolers at their own expense.

I'm almost glad that I was wrong about this market, knowing what I now know about the funding of charter schools. Remember that none of these homeschooled students would have been in school the week they counted noses. Therefore the district isn't receiving any state funding for them. As our "bill" came in, they would have been reducing their allotment from the state for each homeschooled child that enrolled in ECOT. If 80 percent of our students had been homeschoolers, it would have been devastating to the districts that they came from. This payment system has to change, of course, to be fair to the districts.

One reason that I incorrectly thought we would draw from this population was that the parents in these families had already figured out the major question: How do you find the time to homeschool a child and still make a living, care for your home, and have time to sleep? During the time that I was homeschooling my stepdaughter, I saw firsthand the major drain that spending all day with a child has on your energy level and productivity in other areas. It almost has to be the only thing you do. I was working out of my home on my business, and my productivity certainly suffered during that period.

The ECOT model requires that a parent be an integral part of the education team, a teacher's aide of sorts. Parents need to supervise elementary school-aged children or arrange for supervision. Parents need to know enough about their child's assignments at any age to be aware of their child's needs. Do they understand the material? Are they working at a pace that matches their ability? Have they missed something? Do they need to ask the teacher for more help? Should they participate in a chat lesson or attend a field trip? Each student and parent team will arrive at an equilibrium of comfort where both feel that the best outcomes are achieved. Some students need constant reminders; others detest constant supervision. The parent will find out quickly what works.

Most high school students are either home alone during the day or out working. In the latter case, they use their time in the evening to attend school. Their parents become less important as the students develop their own ability to monitor their progress and their work. The parent always has the ability to sign on and see their work immediately. For most high school parents, getting information from their teen about how school is going takes a lot of effort. With

ECOT, the parent and the teacher can have direct communication very easily.

For younger students who require supervision, a working parent might have help from a grandparent or other relative to care for the children while the working parent is at work. Schoolwork can be done in the evening when the parent is at home, with the student completing independent assignments the next day. They could also team up with other ECOT families to share childcare supervision responsibilities.

If all the parents in the household work, it takes an additional ounce of dedication to school a child at home. For many families this effort is worth the additional benefits of a quality education for their child. Most of the families who homeschool their children, through ECOT or not, have given up something in order to do it. Does this make them better parents? Not necessarily. It only makes them parents who have reexamined their personal and family priorities. At the time, children seem to eat up every waking minute, but the 12 years they spend in school account for about 15 to 20 percent of a parent's life, given current life expectancies. Many parents feel that they can refocus on their children for that time and add back other priorities later.

There is another side of this equation that is not often talked about. That is the personal benefit that parents get from being connected to their children and their children's teachers and school. So many of the ECOT parents have shared their fears and frustrations with us. They benefit greatly from knowing that our teachers are their partners in educating their children. We are not going to raise their kids, but we are sympathetic to the struggles that parents experience. When we saw how powerful a force this was in the parent's experience with us, we set out to bring the parents closer to each other. The bulletin boards and chats among parents are very popular and enable them to help each other while we focus on their children.

As the first year unfolded, we found that our market was not parents who had taken the initiative to homeschool their children, but parents who had not yet found a way out. These parents were struggling inside a system that had abandoned their children. We have been focusing on the child's experience, but the parent's is in many ways more critical. To know that your child needs something and not be able to provide it has to be the single most devastating feeling for a parent. The parents who did come to us had been searching, sometimes for years, to not feel as though they had failed their children.

I have noticed something else that happens when parents take an active roll in the formation of their children's education. The cultural environment will shift back toward the family. One of the main reasons we accuse society of not functioning today is the breakup of the nuclear family. When I look back at what I learned throughout all my years of school, the sum total is still less than what I learned from my parents and siblings. I still think that we learn more about the world we live in, maybe not facts and figures, but more about the world from our parents.

Parents need support too as they reverse their role in their child's life. They have insecurities and fears that may not be as easily shared as their angers and frustrations. Rather than criticize parents for not being more involved, the solution is to show them ways to get involved that do not brush up against their own feelings of inadequacy. As their child succeeds, they succeed. Everyone grows stronger.

Graduate Profile:
VERA

There is an old adage that if you want something done, give it to a busy person. Vera is one of those people. The more she has to do, the more she gets done. What we don't often think about is what happens to these people when they aren't given a lot to do. Usually, they get bored and stagnate.

When Vera's family moved to Ashville, a small rural town south of Columbus, she found out exactly how bored someone can be. She had spent the first six years of her schooling moving around the world from military base to military base and attending the base schools for the military brats. People were always coming and going and new friends were easy to come by. The schoolwork was challenging and disciplined.

Ashville was more laid back. The public school didn't have a lot of students like Vera and even though her teachers tried to keep her interested, there was only so much they could do. She knew they couldn't change their whole curriculum just for her. Her grades suffered because she didn't apply herself.

By her junior year, Vera's mother, who had her own data processing business based out of her home, offered to homeschool her. She looked for curriculum and assignments that would keep Vera busy and challenged. Vera immediately applied for a full-time job at a branch bank that opened at the top of her street and did her schoolwork at night. Being busy was good for her, but she found that without the structure of tests and due dates for assignments, she let things go. This caused some friction with her mother.

Her grandfather was the first person in the family to see a news story about ECOT. It seemed that ECOT would give her the one thing she needed from school: structure from a teacher who wasn't her mom. Vera is grateful that her mom tried to help her find a way to learn that would work for her; she knows she must have been a hard student to homeschool.

Vera only needed three courses in order to graduate and move on to a four-year liberal arts college. She was energized by her teachers' interest in each of their subjects and the attention they paid to her. She did miss the social interaction with kids at her high school but found that e-mailing others in ECOT was a lot of fun. It was easier to keep up with her assignments and prepare for tests, even though she was still working full-time at the bank.

As the year went on, she gradually changed her focus to computer technology. She loved everything about the computer: the hardware design, the software applications, and the never-ending possibilities of the Internet. Vera decided to enroll at DeVry Institute of Technology. Her double major in Computer Engineering Technology and Electronics Engineering Technology will allow her tremendous options for career choices.

Vera is taking her time and expects to spend five or six years getting her Bachelor's degree. She wants to keep working and establish her independence at the same time. With one job, two majors, lots of friends, and a love of reading, Vera keeps very busy.

13

KID MAGNETS

"ECOT got me excited about computers.

I took my computer apart and put it back together.

I just had to see how it worked!"

Vera Vest, ECOT Class of '01

Computers have become kid magnets. Just turn one on and watch the kids in a family fight over access to it. Parents have learned quickly that computer time is one of the easiest ways to modify behavior, "No computer time until your room is clean!" The kids start out with games, move on to chats with their friends, and quickly learn how to download music and post cool Web sites.

As computers began appearing in classrooms, there were never enough to go around. Teachers had to ration computer time and students cried foul if they felt they didn't get their fair share. The families who instantly accepted ECOT as a method for delivering education to their children knew that the computer would add a whole new level of excitement to their child's educational experience. Getting their own computer and having all the time on it they want is almost every child's dream.

When a student enrolls in ECOT, he or she immediately receives a packet of printed material to begin working on until their computer arrives. The packet is not as much fun, of course, as the colorful interactive screens that will shortly fill their days. The anticipation builds. When the UPS driver knocks, it's like their birthday. Their present is finally here!

The computers are preprogrammed by Compaq/Xerox to our specifications. The term plug & play is used in electronics these days. Our computers are "plug & learn." With minimal connections, these computers are fully functional within minutes. This assumes that the phone company and the Internet Service Providers have established service for that student. It is an ongoing coordination challenge for our staff to make sure that these three events happen near each other.

The student then switches from the packet of schoolwork to assignments given to him or her at the ECOT online classroom. The developers at Xerox have written millions of lines of code at our direction to make the students' and teachers' experiences online as seamless and integrated as possible.

For the students, the front door to their school is a program that we had Xerox develop called SEP, which stands for Student Electronic Portfolio. When a student signs on, their SEP master page is displayed with some permanent items and most of the information they will need that day. If their teacher or other students have sent them an e-mail message, they will find it here. They will see assignments from all of their teachers, feedback on completed assignments, and announcements about class and school-wide activities.

The teacher's view is similar in that it gathers in one place all their students' activities for the day. They can manage their class from one main screen and then be taken to subsidiary screens for specific tasks to complete, such as assigning work, grading work, scheduling chat sessions, and e-mailing students.

We currently use three main curriculum providers that feed their information to our server in Cincinnati through the Internet: NovaNet, Learn.com, and ChildU. The teachers can combine curricula from each of these providers and hundreds of other approved Web sites that the child can link to from our site. The student will see specific Web page assignments, not unlike a child in a traditional school would be assigned a page in a textbook. If students seem to be having trouble completing the assignments, the teacher can change their assignments to let them have more practice on a particular topic. If a student is completing the assignments quickly and easily, the teacher can add more work or raise the difficulty of the work to match the student's needs.

Other than not meeting their students face to face, the ability to customize curriculum is the biggest difference experienced by our teachers over their previous teaching assignments. In a standard classroom of 25 students, they usually don't have the time to tackle one curriculum, let alone accommodate every student on his or her own path to mastering that subject. One of our curriculum providers actually lets teachers create their own learn centers. And they can locate other sites to supplement or replace the lesson, if they choose. To me, this is the highest respect that any school could pay to a teacher. Allowing teachers to combine their training, expertise, insight, and dedication to teach their students in their own style sets them free to be the best they can. Teaching is a dynamic, creative activity that attracts inventive thinkers to the profession. The more flexibility teachers have, the more they will thrive professionally and the more their students will benefit.

It is amazing to comprehend the amount of curriculum that is already available to us and other electronic schools. This curriculum was developed to serve the market of traditional schools and to use within a classroom environment. More is developed and released every day. Those who select curriculum for school districts know how difficult it can be to choose between competing printed curricula when an entire school district needs to be retooled. Purchasing books and retraining teachers on a new curriculum is a very expensive proposition. Therefore, a lot of care and thought goes into these decisions.

There are two startling differences between printed and electronic curriculum that will totally shake up this selection process for school districts everywhere. First, because an e-course is not printed, it can be changed—and quickly. Especially in the areas of science and social studies, content changes daily as new discoveries are announced and current events change our view of the world. Printed textbooks in these subjects can be outdated before they are shipped. Teachers end up customizing their courses or supplementing the text to correct for the outdated material, which puts more responsibility on their shoulders.

Second, an electronic curricula can be customized to the student and purchased in smaller quantities (down to one) if there is a specific need. An example where this may have a great impact on the quality of education in the country is foreign languages. The laws of economics (yes, schools are businesses) sometimes prohibit less popular foreign languages from being offered. What if a student's parents immigrated from Somalia and the student has learned to speak his family's native language at home but would also like to become literate in that language? Responding to that need could be instantaneous without the district having to purchase printed curriculum in advance and in large quantities.

The vast majority of electronic curriculum providers at this point are small start-up companies. Teachers and writers have seen the demand for these products and have written content in their areas of expertise. What is lacking in the production of these courses is standardization for the purposes of grading and issuing credit. Credits are the measurable outcomes of education. Did the student pass the class? Did the class include a standard amount of work and advancement to count for something? This, of course, has been a long negotiated standard in the field of education. The electronic providers need to join in the game.

This question was one of the first we had to answer as we gave our teachers flexibility in selecting curriculum. And then, as each provider reports results of the coursework completed by the student, how do those results translate into ECOT grades? Several years ago some colleges began giving credit for life experience. If you returned to college after 10 years in banking, you might get five hours of credit toward a basic finance class. It makes sense not to force that student to sit through that required class. However, why shouldn't she get 10 hours of credit? Who determines the equivalencies? Right now we use the SEP program to do this, but the future holds hope for a standardized protocol so we won't have to customize our SEP each time a new provider is added.

Many of the online lessons will suggest hands-on or community experiences for the student to complete with their family. They could also be assigned a book (an old-fashioned paper one) to read or an art project to complete. The percentage of online/offline time the students are spending changes for different ages. Our students might actually spend less time each day in a chair than students in a traditional school. For example, they can choose to participate in over 100 organized field trips a year with other ECOT students. And the number they can complete with their parent is endless. Most students in brick-and-mortar schools can count on one hand the number of trips they get to take in any given school year.

Most people who hear about this new way to deliver education for the first time have a hard time picturing it. They tend to think about the child sitting in front of a computer screen for 6 to 8 hours a day. This has never been the goal, just as it is not the goal in a traditional school for a child to receive 6 to 8 hours of lectures a day. It has been tremendously difficult for the regulators at the Ohio Department of Education to get this image out of their minds. They have attempted to measure a student's attendance rate by the amount of time that he or she is actually online with the school. For some children and some subjects, this may be a very small percentage of their learning time. It is an artificial measurement that has the power to do damage to the student if the teachers are ever encouraged to keep their students glued to their Internet connections. The power of e-schooling is not just the "e" part, but rather how it creates opportunities and efficiencies on top of proven, valuable, learning experiences.

The core curriculum assigned by the teacher looks a lot like any classroom curriculum in a public school in Ohio. The basic skills and subjects are covered. But, unlike most other schools, students as young as Kindergarten can take electives, such as Spanish and Technology. These are not graded and not required, but for the student who would like more challenges, they are great. Keeping the child's interest and providing opportunities to explore are two of the greatest benefits of this delivery system. The parent supervising the younger student will quickly learn what the child is drawn to and may ration their time there so as not to ignore core assignments.

Teacher/student interaction is an area that everyone asks about. How exactly do the teachers teach if they are not physically with the child? The first part of the answer is to remind you that the parent is part of the teaching team. In a standard elementary classroom, a teacher may have 25 students and one teacher's aide or student teacher (if lucky) and various related arts teachers (music, art, phys ed) to fill in during the day. In an ECOT elementary classroom, the teacher may have 50 students and 50 teacher's aides. Other specialized teachers may work with that student online or in their home as well.

Discipline is an interesting issue that we are being forced to address at ECOT. Even though the teachers spend almost no time keeping order (except occasionally refocusing chat sessions) they do have to get the students to do their work. This responsibility falls primarily on the parent. Some students who were never motivated to complete their work at traditional schools bring their habits with them to ECOT and believe that procrastination is easier here. This is an area where we have made many changes and will continue to do so. Our data may show that a student who begins their educational career in an electronic environment will be less likely to have this problem, but we will also get transfer students and need to find a solution.

With virtually no time spent disciplining students, the teacher is free to plan, create, assign, grade, answer questions, run chat sessions, and just plain teach. From the students' perspective, they interact with their teachers six main ways:

- Receiving and sending e-mail messages

- Receiving and sending printed material (at the beginning)

- Participating in chat session lessons

- Phone conversations

- In-person interaction on field trips

- In-person interaction in their home (usually special ed students)

Whereas the kids that ECOT taught had very different educational backgrounds, varying interests and goals, and different overall levels of satisfaction with our program, they all agreed on one thing: the teachers were excellent. Most did not meet even one of their teachers until the graduation ceremony. For some students and teachers, it was an emotional meeting because of the tremendous bond they had developed over the year.

Since they were high school students, they had different teachers for each subject, just as in any high school. They had their favorites, usually aligned with their favorite subjects. The startling difference to them between relationships with teachers earlier in their lives and ECOT teachers was the attention they got. These teachers listened to them, returned their e-mails, took them seriously, and gave them private responses to questions that were not snickered at by 20 classmates. They never felt behind for more than a day on an assignment. They never felt that the teachers did not have time for them.

They remembered that to get private access to a teacher at a traditional school was virtually impossible. Or access was in a very embarrassing setting, like after-school help sessions where others would see that they were having trouble or having to knock on the door of the teacher's lounge. Their question was probably stupid, anyway, so they just skipped it. Very early in their ECOT experience, students stopped skipping over things they didn't understand. It was a new way to learn.

Most colleges now conduct almost all their business using e-mail between professors and students. E-mailing questions is standard fare for most classes. Students from ECOT who are currently in college have moved right into that setting with great comfort. They reported not being afraid to approach professors and get to know them. They e-mail questions and comments regularly to their professors. It is automatic for them.

Chat sessions are another area of great promise for e-learning. Our teachers can hold chats as often as they like and use a variety of formats to engage the students with them. Here is a short example of a chat session with an elementary school Spanish teacher. The text of chat sessions are saved by the teachers or the students for use at any time later. The students don't have to take notes during the sessions as the whole text will be available later.

Elementary chat on colors[1]

Welcome to Learn.com, Inc., JEANNINE_STALLER_184579
Your host is learn.com, running ChatSpace 2.0 - Server Edition
S e r v e r   W e l c o m e
- 7/25/2001 0:15
- Welcome to Learn.com!
This room is recording transcripts
Now talking in 184579
 Welcome to the Chat Room!
Room Moderator in 184579←----JEANNINE_STALLER

←----SPANISH CHAT----→ ¡Hola, this is Sra. Staller!
←----SPANISH CHAT----→ I am glad you are here. Estoy alegre (I am glad)
←----SPANISH CHAT----→ Today we will go over colors.
←----SPANISH CHAT----→ My son (mi hijo) is here, too. His name is Tad. (Se llama Tad).
←----SPANISH CHAT----→ Tad: Hola
←----SPANISH CHAT----→ Tad: hello
←----SPANISH CHAT----→ Hi, Tad! ¿Cómo estás? (How are you?)
←----SPANISH CHAT----→ Tad: I am fine, mamá. Muy bien, mamá
←----SPANISH CHAT----→ negro
←----SPANISH CHAT----→ blanco
←----SPANISH CHAT----→ verde
←----SPANISH CHAT----→ rojo
←----SPANISH CHAT----→ café

←----SPANISH CHAT----→ amarillo

←----SPANISH CHAT----→ anaranjado

←----SPANISH CHAT----→ grís

←----SPANISH CHAT----→ rosado (or rosa)

←----SPANISH CHAT----→ azúl

←----SPANISH CHAT----→ morado

←----SPANISH CHAT----→ These are the colors.

←----SPANISH CHAT----→ The color of the type matches the color of the word.

←----SPANISH CHAT----→ You can go to the Basic Spanish link in the Language Pages course, oral drills chapter, language links page. Here you will find the link to Basic Spanish. On the Basic Spanish site, you will be able to hear the pronunciation of these colors.

←----SPANISH CHAT----→ The game is called: ¿Qué color es? (What color is it?)

←----SPANISH CHAT----→ The question, "¿Qué color es?" is followed by an English word.

←----SPANISH CHAT----→The responder says the color in Spanish of that object. Then, I repeat the object and color in Spanish.

←----SPANISH CHAT----→ Note for Parents: In Spanish the subject and adjective order are reversed. You will also notice that the ending of the noun determines the ending of the adjective.

←----SPANISH CHAT----→ For the purposes of this game at the beginners level, you will only be asked about colors of singular objects. That means one thing, not a group of things.

←----SPANISH CHAT----→ ¿Qué color es un tree?

←----SPANISH CHAT----→ Tad: verde

←----SPANISH CHAT----→ Bueno (good) Un arbol verde (A green tree)

←----SPANISH CHAT----→ ¿Qué color es una banana?

←----SPANISH CHAT----→ Kari: amarillo

←----SPANISH CHAT----→ bueno.... una guinea amarillo.

←----SPANISH CHAT----→ ¿Qué color es un flower?

←----SPANISH CHAT----→ Ben: rosado

←----SPANISH CHAT----→ sí (yes) un flor rosado

←----SPANISH CHAT----→ A flower could be any color really. Probably not black or brown.

←----SPANISH CHAT----→ ¿Qué color es una orange?

←----SPANISH CHAT----→ MacKenzie: anaranjado

←----SPANISH CHAT----→ sí, una naranja anaranjado

←----SPANISH CHAT----→¿Qué color es tu camisa? What color is your shirt?

←----SPANISH CHAT----→ Tad: blanco

←----SPANISH CHAT----→ Kari: negro

←----SPANISH CHAT----→ Ben: blanco

←----SPANISH CHAT----→ MacKenzie: I don't know how to say purple.

←----SPANISH CHAT----→ morado

←----SPANISH CHAT----→ Hay dos camisas blancas

←----SPANISH CHAT----→ There are 2 white shirts.

<----SPANISH CHAT---> Hay una camisa morado... There is one purple shirt.
<----SPANISH CHAT---> Hay una camisa negro....There is one black shirt.
<----SPANISH CHAT---> You can play this game at home with your family. A fun way to play when you are in the car is to name the Spanish color of every car you pass. See if you can come up with the color faster than the cars go past.
<----SPANISH CHAT---> Adiós, amigos
<----SPANISH CHAT---> Good-bye friends.
<----SPANISH CHAT---> Tad: Hasta Luego, amigos.
<----SPANISH CHAT---> Kari: Luego
<----SPANISH CHAT---> Ben: Adios
<----SPANISH CHAT---> MacKenzie: Adios.

Every superintendent in the country will tell you that their job is complicated by the fact that every parent of every child was, at some time in his or her life, a consumer of education services. They know what worked for them and they assume they know what will work for their child. Even more than that, they want their child's education to look just like the one they grew up with. Look how good they turned out, after all. No parent of anyone currently in school could have had an education that looked like this. The technology didn't exist. Anyone who argues that education is best the way it used to be (just because) will be denying their children and grandchildren the excitement of learning in new and magnetic ways that will open up their worlds to material that wouldn't fit in even the largest of school libraries.

NOTES

1. Each word representing a color would appear in that color on the student's computer screen. Also, certain text and/or notes appear in color during chat sessions for more emphasis.

Graduate Profile:
LISA

Rumor has it that Geauga County, east of Cleveland, has more horses per capita than any other county in Ohio. And that's quite all right with Lisa. She spends as much time as possible, sometimes up to 18 hours a day, working with them. What began as a love affair has turned into a career path with just a hint of an obsession.

In seventh grade, Lisa began attending an all-girl private school whose marketing brochure boasts of an on-campus stable. Lisa would spend three months of each school year in Florida training to ride at an important horse show. Her teachers would mail her assignments and she would mail back the work. Lisa had a very early experience with distance learning as a way to allow her to ride at the level she had reached.

As much as she loved her school for giving her the opportunity to ride, she was terribly bored with the academic environment. She wanted something more challenging. Another private school in the area had the reputation of being very rigorous. Lisa transferred and immediately discovered that it was not rigorous enough for her. The school had also told her it would be possible for her to combine her junior and senior years but, once she enrolled, that promise evaporated. By October, Lisa had withdrawn.

Lisa's dad suggested ECOT and it seemed to be the perfect solution.

She could work independently, which she preferred, and travel as much as she wanted to horse shows. When she was out of town, her father would print out the work and send it to her. It didn't feel much different than the arrangement she had had at the private girls' school.

Around the end of March, Lisa realized that she needed only two more credits to graduate and she approached her ECOT advisors with the idea of graduating early. They helped her enroll in the classes she needed and worked with the teachers to provide her with an accelerated schedule in order to complete the courses by graduation.

Lisa had always had the ability to absorb information quickly and disliked learning in a classroom where other students needed repetition. She took a couple of classes last quarter at Kent State and found a similar challenge—independent study is where she thrives. Right now, she's teaching herself Italian. She may look for a Bachelor's program that is taught similarly to ECOT some day.

In the meantime, she enjoys the one-on-one time she spends with the "babies," the two- to three-year-old horses she trains for a living. Through her work experience, Lisa has learned almost all the other aspects of running a horse business—more than any classroom could have taught her.

14

INFINITE CURRICULUM

"With ECOT I accomplished more in less time."

Lisa Darrow, ECOT Class of '01

There are lots of ways to divide the world of learning into curriculum. We tend to put coursework into nice neat packages that make sense to most people. And then something comes along that doesn't fit nicely—or worse—changes our assumptions about how we have been teaching a subject. The biggest example from science is the debate over evolution. Other examples exist in history: Did the Europeans discover America or obliterate an entire civilization of Native Americans? Look at the long road that African-Americans have traveled to even have their ancestor's accomplishments mentioned in the textbooks that document the history of our country.

The goal of all learning should be debate. Ongoing, probing, thoughtful, respectful debate. Never accept the status quo just because someone got past an editor to put some words on paper inside a book. Read more. Ask more. The only problem with much of the curriculum that was developed in previous years is that it stifled debate. Once it was on paper, ready to be memorized and tested, it was very difficult to encourage ongoing examination of the concepts presented. If we haven't taught our children to think for themselves, we are kidding ourselves that we have taught them anything.

So much of the crisis in education has been centered on basic skills, the ones needed to even get to the point where you can begin to debate thoughtful concepts. If you can't read, you can't explore different opinions put forth by those who came before you. If you can't follow a math problem through to its logical conclusion, you won't be able to debate your classmates on the merits of a new concept. It is clear that this issue must be addressed immediately. But we can't rest there.

One of the criticisms waged against the Internet is its Wild West flavor. No fences, no deeds, no roadmaps. Just miles and miles of uncharted information with the possibility of ambush any moment from bad information planted by unsavory characters. You have to be careful, librarians warn. You don't know the source of much of what is out there. But, just like the Wild West, there's gold in them there hills.

The fact that so much information from so many different sources was able to gather in one medium, available at no cost to anyone with an Internet connection at the local library, in such a short period of time is astounding. We are living through it, so it may not seem as grand as it will some day when we look back on this achievement. Compared to the sheer drudgery involved in producing even one textbook for consumption by our nation's students, it's nothing short of a miracle.

Let's compare that textbook to the content on the Internet and catch a glimpse of the next century of curriculum development. By the time a piece of information about the French Revolution makes its way into a fifth-grade history textbook, it has been researched, analyzed, dissected, and generally agreed upon by historians. It has been tested to see whether it offends anyone, confuses anyone, or gives anyone the wrong idea. Then it is combined with other pieces of information that generally round out a lesson to take a standard amount of class time. The student is presented with different ways to process or learn that information: pictures, charts, words, discussion questions, activities, other resources, quizzes, and so on. Then the lessons are bundled together into a history course that might fill a year or half-year of school time.

At the same time that this nugget of history is prepared for presentation in the bound textbook, a historian is sitting in the basement of a library in a little town in France, reading letters from soldiers to their loved ones. He discovers a firsthand account of a battle that contradicts the accepted version. He reads more. He goes back through the historical record that created the accepted version and is certain that this new account is not only accurate but significant in its impact to understand the revolution. He writes a paper for a scholarly journal that is published on the Internet.

Chances are slim that every fifth-grade teacher in the country will read this journal and it will be years before the printed textbooks are able to correct their information. But chances could be very high that the editor in charge of history at an e-curriculum development company does read this journal. She reads the abstract of the article, realizes that this information contradicts the information currently online for her fifth-grade curriculum. And she changes it, adding the citation for her teachers to read if they are interested.

Or, if she feels the information might be controversial or too different from the accepted account that has been taught for years, she might post both versions. This would enhance the student's understanding that our view of history is always changing and that sometimes we have to consider conflicting testimony in our search for understanding.

Now, let's say that French History is offered as an elective to seniors who have completed four years of French language study. This is a very small market compared to the market for fifth-grade history books. The size of the market makes it very expensive for a curriculum publisher to produce and update a text to meet the needs of the students. The costs of e-publishing would allow this curriculum to be available on demand, without printing and stocking the book in advance. The course could be piped into any school in the country through the Internet or distributed on CD-ROM. The information that was added as a sentence or two in the fifth-grade text could be a paragraph with a citation for recommended reading. And an actual picture of the original document that the historian discovered could be included.

Entrepreneurs talk about "time to market." How long does it take from concept design until the customer takes delivery? E-curriculum has the power to take months or years off this measurement, especially for revised texts. Once a printed text is created, publishers prefer to sell the books in their warehouse before they print a new edition. A regular cycle, like three years, may be adopted for revising a popular text. In e-publishing, the cycle could be yearly and would cost less. Certain changes could happen instantly and curricula will probably be rated by their revision cycle. Those with more frequent revisions will be able to charge more to the consumer. This will reduce the teacher's need to adjust or supplement the core curriculum with up-to-date sources.

Teachers always have the prerogative to use pieces of curricula that suit their students and their teaching style. With an e-curriculum, this can be done very effectively. The teacher will be able to "cut and paste" lessons and assignments that flow well with their course design. These enhancements in the production, distribution, and use of curricula are a gift to teachers, who have been handed curriculum for years without the ability to make changes easily. This flexibility also allows the teachers to help the students learn in different directions without disrupting the class or costing excessive amounts of money to purchase different curricula.

As a public school we're confined only to a couple of general rules. Our curriculum must follow or be approved as a state model. For example, the curriculum we use at ECOT is not derived only from pilot state models but also compiled from all 50 states and federal models. There's no sense as a businessperson to cut a path through a forest where you know you're not going to get out the other side. So we have a model that fits. But we have also allowed our teachers to pick one of several different paths that works for themselves and for their students. What we're trying to do is provide a good, basic core curriculum that gets the job done in compliance with those models.

E-schooling has a definite advantage: We can migrate curriculum into areas where traditional schools have difficulty. Here's why. There's been a lot written about textbook companies and what's to be in a textbook and what's not. If you look at recent social studies textbooks that are used by a number of schools throughout the country including Ohio, they devote more time to Marilyn Monroe than to John Kennedy. It's almost as if textbooks have succumbed to the goal of trying to sell books that please an audience rather than trying to tell the true history. There's a lot of revisionism going on.

Think like a textbook company for a minute. They're trying to sell textbooks. They can't print just one. They've got to print 10,000 or 100,000. Then there's a tendency to homogenize curriculum into becoming a plain vanilla flavor. They also have a tremendous lobbying force with the departments of education across the country so that in order to provide a cost-effective way of providing the textbooks, the Ohio Department of Education has to give in a little bit to the textbook manufacturer.

Textbook writers have to project what they think the demand will be. They do this by surveying schools and doing extensive market research, but it is still a risk. Government-run schools will rarely send out Requests for Proposals (RFPs) asking for an entirely new curriculum or textbook to be developed just for them. But we can do that. As a business, we can guarantee a relationship that is not subject to bid. We can request customized curricula that developers can price at profitable margins and know they are developing a customer relationship. This is not possible the way school districts currently do business. You don't see them creating a vision of what they want and then asking a provider to do it, whereas you see business doing it all the time. Business people are used to picking up the phone and asking, "Hey, can you get this done for me?" We can craft, experiment, and create with the vendor as a partner. We are now looking at ways to not necessarily buy what they have but to motivate them to create what we need. A needs-based curriculum develops where our students have a need that is fulfilled more easily than traditional models of curriculum development.

Instead of a bound volume that quickly goes out of date and was never a real-time book, electronic textbook publishing can produce real-time books. The publishing industry will find their products will no longer be sold, but leased. Instead of buying a textbook, we lease content by the day. We buy whatever we use from a knowledge base that publishers maintain for us. The worlds of journalism and curricula writing will merge. Curriculum will include journalistic input that ties areas of the curriculum to events of the day and discoveries of the hour. Learning will be exciting to children in a way it has never been, because it will be relevant and real to them.

Taking this to the next logical level, this technology will allow for cross-curriculum courses. We can take curricula from multiple textbooks to create a new paradigm of real-time studies that ties science, economics, history, or whatever the student and the teacher need to complete the understanding of the lesson. There's clearly a belief that when you begin to teach children in this way, they learn more. How do you apply what you learn in math to what you learn in history to what you learn in English? When you put in place those kind of efforts, a better learning process is going on. It is cumbersome to try to accomplish this in the current world of scheduled classes and printed textbooks. E-schooling will allow us to take parts of topics and combine them more easily than ever while never having to buy a textbook.

In order for this to work, curriculum developers will have to make money. Right now, they know how to take an order, ship a book, and submit an invoice. They understand that. If we have 30 students, we need 30 books. We pay for 30 books and they make the profit they need to stay in business and develop the next book we need. Software suppliers have been selling their products by the use of licenses. This is a little more problematic. Everyone probably has at least one piece of software that someone "loaned" them. No license was purchased and no money went to the developer. This can only work for a while, until the developers leave to work in another industry where they can get paid for their work.

When we start talking about leasing content, we are moving even farther away from concepts that are currently in practice and easily understood. Remember when you were a kid and the new multiplex theaters were built? It didn't take you and your friends long to figure out that you only had to pay once and you could hang out all day, going from show to show. Your parents probably loved it. It was a place to park you where you would get in the least amount of trouble and it was cheap. This is the fear of most content developers. You pay once and use it over and over, leaving them with no profit margin to stay in business.

What if, instead, when you enter the theater you are given a smart card that you swipe each time you go into a show and you pay on the way out based on the number of swipes your card racked up while you were there? This is the philosophy of how the use of curriculum will work in the future. Xerox has developed a product called Content Guard that counts those swipes. It will allow us to load a curriculum product on our server for little or no money and only pay when a student uses it. The curriculum supplier would need to trust the validity of the Content Guard data, but the idea is to not force the suppliers who are developing good products out of business. If we place a product on our server and none of the teachers like it or assign it, that producer may need to rethink their product. It is a true market-driven system. This is the type of technology that will allow schools to lease very small units of curriculum and give the suppliers the incentive to produce them.

Let's say you have thousands of little software developers or even big ones and they're all writing code. The key will be when the e-schooling business gets big enough to establish itself as a real industry with standards. What we can do then is drive the equation and say to a curriculum developer that if you want to provide a new course that we need, that's wonderful. We like your course, we like the graphics, we think it'll work. You will now write it to code that fits our distribution channel. They will love it because they know that their product will "fit" on the shelf. It can carry with it standardized grading and credit reporting so that the schools can take student results and feed them directly into their reporting system. That is where we are headed.

What we are talking about totally decentralizes the control of curriculum. Current educators were weaned on the model where the elementary principal who is tired of being a principal gets "promoted" to an office at the school board and given the power to select curriculum. She reads and researches, compares and contracts, surveys and scans, and voilà! A curriculum appears. The teachers are trained and coerced into using it. It makes things simple for the district. One textbook. One input to measure against the output of the standardized scores. So simple.

In electronic education where you are now breaking textbooks down into microbytes, you empower teachers to become real curriculum advisors. In other words, they're teaching to the child's desires, wants, and needs, as they support the parents' preferences for their children's education. You can create 50 different scenarios in which that material is taught. You can give parents options on controversial subjects like evolution and sex education. You can help students explore their heritage as a second-generation American from a country that would never make it to a one-size-fits-all American social studies textbook. You have infinite possibilities. You can encourage debate and individual thinking. You can end up with educated, not just programmed, people.

Graduate Profile:
JENNIFER

Jennifer still wears her golden hair long — just like the golden strands in the story of Rumplestiltskin. That was the first book she was able to read all by herself. It was an emotional moment that still excites her 10 years later! She was older than most children when she first experienced that thrill due to learning disabilities that were not diagnosed until halfway through the third grade.

For the first three and a half years at Deshler Elementary in the Columbus Public School District, Jennifer fought to keep up with the other students. In third grade it became obvious to everyone that she was losing the battle. She was bringing home more and more of her work that she couldn't finish during the allotted class time.

Her teacher and her mother had very different explanations for her work patterns. Her teacher accused her of goofing off and not caring about her work. Her mother asked why her daughter couldn't learn like the rest of the children. She knew her daughter was trying. Jennifer knew she wasn't goofing off. In fact, she knew she was trying twice as hard as any other student. She didn't understand why it was so hard for her to understand what the other students seemed to grasp quickly. She would put pressure on herself to do something but that seemed to slow her down even more.

After her mother asked for Jennifer to be assessed, the school first tried some classroom strategies and then assigned her a tutor. The tutor's help frustrated Jennifer even more because now she knew she could learn if someone took the time to work with her. The other 90 percent of the time, she continued to struggle.

Her mother continued to battle for Jennifer to be placed in the learning disability classroom. Halfway through the year, she succeeded. It was like night and day for Jennifer. She was so happy to be with other students who understood her situation and with a teacher who had the time to work with her. The teacher used teaching strategies that worked well for Jennifer's disability. She continued with the same curriculum that her former classroom was using, just delivered in a way that allowed her to learn at her own pace. She also had the benefit of working with the same teacher for the following two school years.

The next year at middle school, Jennifer was placed in the learning disabled class, which continued to work well for her. She took her academic subjects with two LD teachers and joined the rest of her class for music, art, and physical education. For the first time, she was able to see the "normal" kids pick on other students for being "stupid" or claiming that their classroom had "padded walls." She remembers how they insulted each other by insinuating that they were in the LD class, even if they weren't. She learned to keep to herself and not make it known that she actually was in the LD class.

Jennifer had lifelong friends from her neighborhood who formed the foundation of her social life. They knew that she was in a special class but didn't care. Her family provided a good base as well. Jennifer found emotional and social support from them that she didn't find at school.

By high school, Jennifer had formed some friendships outside of her LD classmates, but was still hiding the fact that she had learning disabilities. Her friends just thought she had different classes than they did. And she wasn't about to tell them differently.

Jennifer heard about ECOT from her aunt who had decided to enroll her children in our school. Jennifer initially made the decision to transfer for a very unselfish reason but then found that it was beneficial for her as well. Jennifer's mother was in remission from cancer, but still had restrictions on her activities. She was raising a very active four-year-old grandson and Jennifer thought that if she stayed home to do her schooling, she could help with her nephew's care.

She designed her school schedule around his meals and naps. She broke up her work into several small chunks to fit around the times when her mother could supervise the child. Then she would prepare his meals and give him his bath each day. She has maintained her role in his life and is grateful for the opportunity to help both her mother and her nephew.

Jennifer points to several benefits from this arrangement for herself. At the top of the list are the appreciation she feels and the boost her self-esteem has taken for being able to contribute to the needs of others. She has also learned some valuable life skills including food preparation and child care.

Her experience at ECOT was similar to her LD classroom experience, but enhanced. ECOT gave the same attention to her specific learning style and she received similar individual attention from her teachers. What was missing was the pressure to perform in front of other students and the worry about feeling stupid or being made fun of. She felt even more freedom to be herself and to learn on her own terms with total support from her teachers.

Jennifer is happy with her life right now. Continuing to help raise her nephew and working as a waitress take up most of her time. She is saving up to get her own place and begin her life as an independent adult. She is not thinking about continuing her education in an official manner. She is realistic about her learning disability and knows that many careers that require education beyond high school might be too much pressure for her. The main lessons that her education taught her are to take things slowly and to trust herself. Jennifer is content to be reading Rumplestiltskin to her nephew, and that's the most important thing she could be doing right now.

15

RINGING THE SCHOOL BELL CURVE

"If a child says they can't learn, try to understand why."

Jennifer Perkins, ECOT Class of '01

Every child is unique. We want to believe this, but the reality is that some are more unique than others. The world of public education thinks not in straight lines but in bell curves. The school bell rings the loudest in the middle of the curve. Those students who walk the walk and talk the talk of mainstream America are those best served by the public education system. Those at the ends of the curve are left to fare for themselves all too often—maybe because of limited resources, maybe because of a lack of specialized teachers, or maybe because the problems faced by public schools have overwhelmed the delivery of services to the "normal" kids, let alone to these exceptional children.

The term exceptional has been used to define those students at the two ends of the curve. They are the exceptions to the rule that students will learn well in the environment delivered by public education in brick-and-mortar buildings on set schedules using commonly available teaching tools. In a child's early years, much of the education system's goal is to help him or her become comfortable with that delivery system. Punish them if they are late. Reward them if they sit still and pay attention. Make them uncomfortable if they lag behind or exceed the pace of the rest of the class. Give them a sticker if they go through the motions.

Molding the child to the education rather than molding the education to the child has been the cost-effective way to deliver education for several generations. Keeping the child in the regular classroom has been the ultimate goal. Once a child has to be pulled out and given special attention or special programming, costs skyrocket. Regular classroom teachers have classes that are too large to design individual programs or give the needed individual attention to each unique learner. New strategies are circulating that can help the more creative teachers address this issue of a variety of learners, but students at the very ends of the curve will still need special attention.

Parents of both learning disabled and gifted children know very early how the bell curve works. Many times they become directly involved in the interventions that their children need to progress. When our phones began ringing off the hook, it was these parents who surprised us. We knew that the additional money available to school districts to serve these children and the small class sizes would be attractive reasons for the parents to continue in their neighborhood school. What we didn't know was how many children were on the fringe of these programs and had not been allowed in. The small rural school districts where funding is already tight had problems keeping up with the demand for these services.

It also became clear that some parents had limited abilities themselves, possibly as a result of the same treatment during their educational experience, and could not be effective advocates for their children. They found that the system was just too difficult to navigate and roadblocks were firmly in place. They would buckle under the pressure of their own ineffectiveness, their child's growing frustration, and the school's lack of responsiveness to their problem. Those parents who did have the communication and negotiation skills to fight the system might be labeled as troublemakers and end up nowhere as well. So they were calling us. As a group, they became some of our strongest supporters in this first year.

We began a Department of Exceptional Children immediately and welcomed these children and their frustrated parents with open arms. It is hard to think of these students as having something in common that qualifies them to be served by a special division of ECOT. In fact, it is their differences that define them, not their similarities. Exceptional children can be gifted or talented in one area while experiencing a severe learning disability in another. They may be ahead intellectually and way behind their age cohorts behaviorally. They may be in the bell curve of the learning ability but suffer with a physical disability that prevents them from attending a brick-and-mortar school.

The ECOT model is based on the team approach used by public schools and funding primarily by the federal government through title grants. The team is composed of the regular education teacher, the special education teacher, tutors, special needs consultants, and, most importantly, the parent of the student. The student is the center of attention in this team approach. The team looks for the best strategy that will work for the student.

The technological advances that serve the vocational rehabilitation field and adult mental retardation/developmental disabilities field are just sitting there waiting to be applied to younger populations. Different computer technologies for user interface, such as a mouse easier to use by people with motor control problems or voice control software, open up the world of information to students with physical disabilities. Special reading software allows blind students to interact with their computers. And the list goes on. If a student has a physical, mental, or learning disability, odds are good that there are solutions waiting to be installed in their home. Our staff of trained specialists is constantly researching and receiving training on the latest technologies that might help our students.

Many of these students receive regular home visits from our teachers and tutors. Those who were previously prevented from attending a brick-and-mortar school due to medical issues are finding the attention a great improvement over what their local school district was able to offer them. Often the teachers and tutors are working with parents to give them skills to work with their child during the rest of the week. Ongoing contact is provided through the computer and over the phone.

ECOT has the same challenges as other public schools in determining which students will benefit from this type of approach. And as with other schools, it is not cheap. We receive federal grants to fund the additional services these students receive and therefore need to follow the various procedures required to place a child in this type of program. Even though this money adds to our revenue, it is instantly used up with the direct costs of servicing that child and may not come in until months after the child is placed in the program. During the 2001–2002 school year, there were 350 students who had qualified for our exceptional needs programming, but the Federal Government was sending us grants for only 135. This delay in receiving funds puts a huge financial strain on all schools. Because the regulations dictate that services must be provided as soon as a child is assessed, many districts will delay the assessment process as long as possible.

Usually, in any school, the teacher and principal will notice that a child is having a problem and will look for a classroom intervention that might help. Some children who come to ECOT find that their problems are instantly minimized due to the individual attention they receive from both their classroom teacher and their parents. In addition, the ability to work at their own pace may be all the change they need. For some, the lack of pressure from classmates and the quiet environment of their home allow them to focus on their work.

If the problem persists or has already been assessed in their old school, the student is then placed in the Exceptional Children program and the intervention intensifies. The testing is the same as at any school in Ohio. It consists of a complete psychological exam, which is different from a mental health assessment. It measures the child's intellectual capabilities. Then we do an academic assessment, which is compared to the child's measured abilities.

The difference between these two results often alerts us to a problem. If a child has a higher-than-average intellectual capability and a lower-than-average academic achievement, we do further testing to try to determine why the child isn't learning to his or her ability and what intervention is indicated.

A basic neurological exam measuring visual motor integration might give us the answer. We also do a test called the Adaptive

Behavior Assessment and the Conner's Rating Scale, which help discover attention deficit hyperactivity disorder. We ask the parents to have the child take a complete physical from a physician and we look for hearing and vision problems.

Many of these tests are as important to help rule out various problems as to rule them in. The more we rule out, the closer we get to knowing what types of educational strategies will be the most likely to succeed with the child. It is certainly not an exact science and may require a period of trial and error. With the parent as part of the intervention team, however, the feedback is immediate, allowing the professionals to adjust and refocus the treatment to better serve the child.

As all the testing is completed, we gather the results and all the parties involved for a meeting called a Multi Factored Evaluation (MFE). We have all the reports in writing or in person from the psychologist, the academic tester, the hearing specialist, the occupational therapist, and any others that have been ordered. The regular teacher, the special education teacher, the counselor, the principal, the parent and the child (if he or she is over 12) are part of the meeting. The child has a right to know his or her educational plan and to have a say in it. This evaluation is done every three years.

On a yearly basis, another plan called an Individual Education Plan (IEP) is completed and used to guide the team for that school year. Using IEPs allows students to progress at their own rate, emphasizing areas of concern and allowing them to progress to their own maximum level of functioning. If we have a student enroll who is already 14 years old and not yet reading at a fourth-grade level, the IEP will be very different from the IEP of a student who is reading well at that age but doesn't retain anything he or she reads.

We review the results at these meetings trying to make sure that the parents understand as much as possible. Depending upon the education level and age of the parents, this can be a challenge.

Remember that the parents may have been educated by the same system that is failing their children, and not that many years ago. The children may be dealing with the same social, environmental, and genetic influences that their parents were faced with. Our goal is to stop the pattern with this generation, giving the child the educational interventions that the parents may not have had available to them. Our teachers find that parents appreciate the special attention given to them as well. As adults they are very aware of their own learning abilities and welcome an opportunity to speak frankly about their own frustrations with education.

Another problem for some of these families is the lack of access to medical care due to low income or lack of insurance. ECOT has paid for several physical examinations when the family could not afford it. It is so important to the well-being of the child and the effectiveness of the educational plans to know what we're dealing with. If there is a medical condition that needs treatment and prevents the child from learning, we need to know. We currently have 40 percent of our families officially at or below the poverty level. Another 20 percent is suspected, but they have not completed the forms in order for us to be able to identify them in this population. This level of income makes the routine visit to the doctor a significant cost to the family.

Testing for gifted children is exactly the same as for learning disabled children. In fact, it is rare to find a child who is gifted in all areas. Some, in fact, may have a hidden disability that they mask with their gifted behavior in other areas. Or it is ignored, because he or she is such a "good student" in most areas. Einstein is reported to have been dyslexic without the ability to read for many years, but his genius in math and science was well documented. This pattern is more common than you might think.

Another problem that many gifted students face is a general delay in social skills. The teasing that many academically advanced students face in school is more devastating because they don't have the same social maturity that their less intelligent peers possess. So we are looking for an understanding of the whole child and any issues that might be keeping them from performing to their abilities. In the traditional public school, the approach to these problems is to categorize a student as one or the other, gifted or disabled. It is virtually impossible to get services at both ends of the spectrum.

The main issue for many gifted children is pacing. If a subject is mastered in half the time of the rest of the class, the probability of boredom is high. With boredom often comes behavior problems and a lack of motivation. The ECOT self-paced curriculum by definition eliminates this issue. Students are individually assigned work that will keep them challenged and help them explore their own interests, while not allowing them to ignore areas that may be more difficult. In a regular classroom, the quick advancement of a student presents social problems. It is not inherent in the public school system to allow students to learn in multi-age environments. Students are encouraged, almost mandated, to stay with their age cohorts.

That is not how we are choosing to handle the situation. A student will start with us at the grade level he or she advanced to in their last school setting. Each teacher will assign work that is appropriate for that student's rate of advancement. If the student is identified as exceptional, a special needs teacher is also assigned to that student to work on areas of need. Their classroom teacher will maintain the records and supervise their education, relying on the special needs teacher to provide the special intervention, which might be at-home or library visits, daily phone contact, and other resource management.

One of the more difficult things we have to do is make sure that the supervision of the child is appropriate. There is an issue throughout the ECOT learning experience about what age a child can or should be left alone for even part of a day. We expect that our high school students and some middle school students are safe when home alone, if their parents are at work. But with a special needs child, especially one who is medically fragile, that may not be the case. Many of our families are also receiving services from county Health, Mentally Retarded/Developmental Disabilities (MR/DD), and Mental Health agencies, so we have case managers and social workers who can assist us in this effort. We know that these families are constantly under a great deal of stress and we are attempting to be a partner in helping relieve that stress, not add to it. Sometimes, however, we need to report abuse and neglect and that is a very sad day. This intervention may actually result in a family receiving the respite care that they need or other ongoing visiting services from county agencies.

These partner agencies are beginning to see e-schooling as a marvelous option for many of their consumers. The educational component of a child's case management plan is always important, although the local schools may not have the resources to customize a plan for an individual student. Allowing the social workers to be part of the planning process, we can arrive at new and creative solutions for the student. Large cities may have long-established programs and workshops for MR/DD populations, but rural areas may not have the resources to provide the same level of service. Some students may be referred to vocational rehabilitation programs and attend those programs for part of the day or be placed in a sheltered job within their community.

The power of e-schooling for students who hang by a thread at the ends of the bell curve is only beginning to be exposed. As the teacher shortage continues, the country is expecting a critical shortage in special needs teachers. Their valuable expertise will need to be used in the most efficient manner possible. Specialists in the medical field work with a team of delivery personnel below them. We may eventually have to use special education teachers in the same way. They would be essential to customize curriculum and supervise progress, but may have to rely on regular classroom teachers, social workers, and parents to be the delivery system. The e-schooling model accommodates this potential shortage automatically.

There is nothing more personally rewarding than to watch a student who couldn't learn before begin to learn. The pure joy in their eyes and the sense of accomplishment is unmatched. It takes a special person to enter the field of special education and I am so proud of our entire team of teachers who have dedicated their professional lives to this niche of educational excellence. They are rewarded every day from the students' advancements. Yet they are also dealing with the ongoing frustrations of a public education system that doesn't honor the inherent worth of these students as human beings. The teachers are also exceptional human beings and I will keep fighting for their ability to deliver the best possible education to this special group of children.

Graduate Profile:
WENDY

Like many kids today, Wendy grew up in two different worlds. The one at home, where the rules were set by her grandparents. And the one at school, where the rules were a little fuzzy. Wendy felt that she could deal with her friends and their choices while being smart and keeping herself out of trouble. Her grandparents didn't agree.

They had raised Wendy since birth in a suburb of Columbus. She attended both Catholic and public schools. She enjoyed school and did well academically. Her grandparents trusted her but didn't trust her friends. The type of trouble her friends could find didn't even exist when they were teens. But they knew how important it was for teenagers to "fit in."

Looking back, Wendy knows they did the right thing to separate her from her peers and enroll her at ECOT. At the time, she felt as if she had been sentenced to ECOT. However, her eyes were focused on that diploma and nothing was going to keep her from graduating. If she couldn't graduate with her class, she was going to graduate at ECOT. Whatever it took.

Little did she know how much it would take. The frustration level was high, as her equipment didn't work at first and she had to do many of her assignments on paper. She remembers being shocked each time she could actually get online. She would play "beat the clock" to print out as much as she could while the server was up. This way she would have something to do when the server was down, which for her it usually was.

Wendy remembers a really horrible day when she had a book report due on a novel. She worked for hours to get it done on time and signed on to turn it in. E-mail was down. She drove several miles to the ECOT office to turn it in so that she would get the grade she needed to graduate. The letters G.E.D. were not in her vocabulary.

It is this ability to cope with the challenge of the moment that immediately separated Wendy from her new peers: her coworkers at National City Bank. As the youngest member of her team, she works in the Online Banking Department answering calls from customers who cannot get online! She is rewarded with wonderful evaluations and nice raises. She loves her job and her coworkers. She feels fortunate to be working for such a great company. They gave her over two months of classroom training when she started and inspired her to learn more. Wendy sees herself running a department like this someday. The world of call centers and technical support is where she wants to stay.

Listening to agitated people all day long is not the idea of a fun job to most 19-year-olds. Wendy copes with the situation by explaining that she knows she can help them. Sometimes she needs to wait for callers to blow off some steam before they will listen, but eventually she can solve their problem. She credits her trainers and supervisors for giving her the tools to accomplish this. She knows that a lot of folks are still getting used to using computers and the Internet. She feels that ECOT let her start out her career ahead of the game, with skills that many people don't have.

Wendy knows that she needs much more education in order to move up in a company like NCB. She is studying for an Associate's degree in Business at Columbus State Community College. Their program is very flexible for working students and the cost is affordable. She describes her business classes as the kind that fit her. Other classes aren't so automatic, but she knows that her degree will lead to other opportunities. Once again, she has her crystal green eyes focused on graduation.

16

ECOT'S EARLY HURDLES

"It was hell while it lasted, and heaven at the end
when I got that diploma."

Wendy Napier, ECOT Class of '01

I once heard a speaker at a conference for entrepreneurs share an interesting insight. You don't solve problems in business with the goal of not having any more problems. You solve problems so that you will be a little better at solving the next problem that comes along. Because they will.

It's a little overwhelming to look back over all the problems we have solved and put them together on the pages of this book. We attacked them one at a time, each day reacting to the crisis of the moment. Even though many of them were happening simultaneously, the only way to get through is to set priorities and attack the one that is the most threatening or the closest to a solution on any given day. Then wake up the next day and attack the next one.

There will never be another ECOT, another school that is the first to bring K–12 e-schooling to Ohio. Many of the problems that we dealt with will never recur here, but they could be repeated in state after state until the revolution is complete. When the concept is no longer news and the business model matures, the problems will be different. The problems we overcame were unique, but not necessarily more daunting than the struggles faced by any new concept.

In America, business has reached a level of tremendous success. We have figured out how to prepare the exact same hamburger at every freeway exit in the country to the exact same standards and for nearly the same price. This is nothing short of amazing, but we have forgotten how many years ago Dave Thomas struggled to get his first restaurant off the ground here in Columbus. We have no patience for quality to develop. We expect perfection right out of the gate. Or, at least, we don't want to know what's going on in the kitchen.

With respect to another Dave with staying power, I offer you my Top 10 List of ECOT's Early Hurdles:

10. No Models or Benchmarks to Follow

During an early meeting with Mike Bradley, my finance guru, we were making a feeble attempt at a business plan. He threw his pen down and exclaimed, "I don't think we should plan too much. There's no way. I have made 10,000 commercial loans and I've never seen anything like this. Bill, you have the beginning of a business that never existed before. It may be the beginning of an industry. It is so complex and there are so many variables and unknowns that if we do any planning, it won't fly. Let's do it on a napkin, let's sell, sell, sell, and do the planning later. If you sit down and try to account for your special needs, money, funding, and all that, it blows your mind."

That isn't exactly the reaction you'd expect to hear from a banker. So I asked him, "Mike, you want to jump the cliff?" He said, "Yeah. This is the craziest thing. I never in my life ever thought I would see an idea that I would say, lend money to it without a financial statement." The power of the idea was so much stronger than any business model that existed. We had to throw our hearts into it first and let our minds follow.

Without models and benchmarks, we were really operating on faith. If we had looked at all the complications of this school, we would have been insane to attempt it halfheartedly. It was all or nothing. So there's a little bit of cliff jumping going on. We're standing at the edge of a cliff: Do we do it or do we not? It's a real toss-up because you don't know the truth and it became "What the hell, let's jump!" Entrepreneurs are often described a lot of different ways. To me, it comes down to one basic quality that is almost a suicidal quality because as such, it's done with passion and abandon. If you lack that passion, it won't succeed. If you have the passion, you get to go to the next step.

9. Initial High School Curriculum Was Untested

In our shopping for curriculum, we looked at a very impressive

Web-based program for middle school and high school. We bought it for three times what other curricula would cost us in the future. We didn't know that we were seeing a little guinea pig prototype when we tested it. We didn't know that our students were going to be their guinea pigs. It was a beta test, if it was that far along in its development. It caused us headaches from day one and the promises to fix it grew old quickly. As well, they underestimated our needs and market size and could not keep up, especially since they had misrepresented the capabilities of their program from the start. Obviously, that's not what we wanted. Having to switch midstream and say, "It's not working" was a very difficult job. Everyone had to be retrained. The students had to adjust. As I suspected, if I needed to get a new curriculum, I could. I just didn't know how soon I would be asked to make that decision and how much disruption it would cause.

8. Phone Bill Costs and Lost Computers

One of the variables that would have been very hard to put into an initial business plan was shrinkage. Every business has it. Inventory walks out the door. Employees use company assets for personal use. Things break. In our case, we never imagined that the students would be as costly in this line item as they are.

One thing that caught us off guard was long distance charges. We own the phone lines that are installed in the students' homes and they are not set up with long distance service. However, kids know about 10-10 calls to get around long distance blocks. We have been arguing with the local phone companies to take the ability to make 10-10 calls off the students' phones, but regulations about limiting competition are getting in our way.

Another shocker was how many computers we would lose. Our database tracking the computers did not work properly for several months and we did not have good follow-up processes in place to retrieve computers that were no longer being used. The families seemed very happy to just hold on to the asset without doing their part to get it back to us. We had a system with our supplier: whenever a computer needed to be returned, a UPS prepaid label was sent to the family. They needed to box it up and call UPS. When they did not follow through, we didn't know.

7. Start-Up Capital

By our count, we had 3 million dollars of operating and financial losses during our first year in business. The amount of money we lost is the exact amount of money it must have required to capitalize the business properly. By the way, we acquired 6 million in assets during the same time period. When you have an undercapitalized business, you are forced to use money that should go to operating expenses to capitalize the business. Everything from the water cooler to the electronic infrastructure of the school was paid for out of current revenue. We didn't lose 3 million dollars—we know exactly where it is, working hard to keep this school running as capital invested in the business.

6. Timeline

Follow these dates for a moment. We got our charter the first of April 2000. We would not receive funding until the third week in July. We had to start school September 1st. So from April 1st through September 1st, we needed servers, program code written, facilities, teachers, and curriculum. We also had to develop and staff the marketing effort. Our round-the-clock effort then became how do we pull all these corporate sources, friends, and supporters of ECOT together to build the first ever Internet school with no money and knowing that when we got money, the school had to open up 30 days later. That's almost impossible. Envision opening up a high school and saying you have 30 days to build a school, enroll the students, hire the teachers, and have all the reporting systems together. That is what the state of Ohio requires of its charter schools.

5. Conflict Between Businesspeople and Educators

We had a civil war about halfway through our first year. On one side were the educators and on the other side were the business people. Those two camps had admittedly had very little experience working side-by-side with the other professional perspective. My pro-business attitude really irritated the educators. My notion that the business had to be strong in order to support a strong educational environment created an atmosphere that they had never encountered. Many of our other problems were blamed on the fact that I am not an educator by training.

Several of the educators left. This caused a temporary upheaval, although excellent people moved right into their positions and established a better environment for everyone to co-exist. Other e-schools that have been attempted in Ohio have not shown nearly the success we have—probably for the reason that they have not paid enough attention to the business side of the equation.

Educators who grow up professionally in a public school environment, where there is no such thing as going out of business, understandably have no instinct for what makes a business survive and thrive. Their skills are invaluable to deliver a quality product, but they can't be expected to run a business when the margins are so close.

4. Anxious Market Demanding Perfection

Without our knowledge, the day before our charter was issued, the media learned of our charter. The announcement hit the papers across the state and calls began flooding into the State Department of Education. I remember getting home that night about two in the morning and checking my caller ID. There were calls from all the Ohio area codes: 419, 216, 330, 513, 947, and on and on. Amazingly, the Department of Education was giving out my home phone number.

My phone rang around the clock for two weeks straight. Late one night, after a day and night of nonstop meetings, I came in the door to hear my phone ringing. I tried to ignore it, took a shower, and fixed a snack. It was after one and the phone was still ringing. Instead of turning off the ringer and going to bed, I answered it. It was a mother from near Toledo, "I'm so glad I got hold of you. I've had you on automatic redial for two days. I need you to take my son. He really needs to come to your school. We don't have any other options for him. Can you hold for a minute?" Before I knew it she had her neighbor on three-way calling with us, telling me about her child. Then the next neighbor was conferenced in. And the next. There I was, talking to 10 moms from Toledo at two in the morning.

It was about this time that we knew we had a monster. We had no enrollment forms, no furniture, no phone system, but we had customers. Waiting customers. Anxious customers. And lots of them. Our notion was that we would get ready and then go looking for them. But they found us way before we even flirted with the notion of being ready. Complaints started pouring into the Department of Education: they won't return my calls, they won't let me register my child. It was a nightmare. The worst that could have happened was to hold out hope to a parent who had lost hope and then cause them more disappointment. That was certainly not in the business plan.

3. Ohio Department of Education (ODE) Roadblocks

I could complain that ODE didn't provide adequate training and information to effectively begin a charter school, but that wouldn't be a fair complaint. They are new at this too and we certainly presented a revolutionary concept that they couldn't have known how to handle in advance. So I will give them that benefit of the doubt. What I didn't expect, though, was misleading information, constantly changing rules, auditors in my office year-round, and payment policies that caused every superintendent in the state to want to slash my tires.

We have been paid differently from any school before us, been given different formulas to measure our student body, and had money withheld from our payments with no explanations and no appeal. Our federal grant funds have been delayed for up to eight months with no explanation. I could go on. After a while you start to get the message that somebody doesn't like you.

We know that we had start-up problems. What is not excusable is that our State Department of Education chose to be one of our problems instead of helping us find solutions. However, I know that holding us to higher standards than other schools and subjecting us to constant audits will only make us stronger in the long run.

2. Computer Shipments and Server Challenges

Time was not on our side as we began the school. We were writing our own system (Student Electronic Portfolio) at the same time we were building the servers. We didn't give ourselves adequate time to test their compatibility in the first couple of months. Jerry Margeson gets the duct-tape-and-bubble-gum award for keeping the system together during this very tenuous period.

For the student's computers, we chose the Windows 2000 operating system, which had only been out a matter of weeks before we needed to begin installing it. It was full of bugs, which we had to cope with along with everything else. We also chose a printer/scanner multifunction device that didn't work. Students couldn't scan their work until April, which affected mostly the elementary students. We eventually replaced all the printer/scanners.

Getting the equipment to the students was initially a logistical nightmare. The student first needed to officially enroll allowing us to order his or her computer. The leasing company had a lag time to set up the lease on that specific equipment. We then got behind on building up the machines because of the huge demand that we had not anticipated.

1. Media Attention

One evening I was the last person to leave our newly rented space in Southland Mall. It was very late at night. As I walked out into the parking lot, I saw my car and, a couple of rows over, an unmarked van with two men sitting in it. I was a little nervous. I got my cell phone ready to call 911 in case this turned into a problem. As I walked quickly to my car, I heard, "Sir, sir! May we talk to you? We're TV reporters, can we take a moment of your time?" They had a camera and were ready to interview me.

We had been doing about 100 interviews a week and had three people assigned to do nothing but field requests from the media, yet these guys wanted to talk to me. They were three hours away from home, sitting in a deserted parking lot in the middle of the night to get the story. The only problem was that there wasn't a story. Not yet, anyway.

In the world of public relations, there is a term called "earned media." It's free coverage by the media that brings attention to your business or event or discovery. At the time that we were being hounded by reporters from all over the state, we hadn't "earned" anything. I would call this more accurately "found media." This was the type that happens when you win the lottery. Even though you are happy you won, you wish the media would go away and let you enjoy your winnings.

Or, in our case, build our business. We certainly had every intention of sending out numerous press releases when we were ready to announce our school and begin attracting students. In fact, we were counting on it, knowing that money would be very tight to purchase advertising.

In a strange way, by jumping the gun the media began the cycle of challenges. They raised expectations in the minds of parents, who immediately expected to find a school ready to serve their children. When they didn't find that, they complained to the State Department of Education, who then had the justification they needed to come after us, which then gave the media a story they could chew on. The media coverage that followed has been very critical, to the point of digging up my past personal life and leaving us very tired of wondering what will be printed next.

No other business, school, or government agency could have survived the incessant scrutiny by the media that we endured for an entire year. We have no secrets and no possibility of a moment of privacy. We live in a glass house with everyone looking in. Some days and some media articles were harder than others, but I am most sad for the kids who were going to school during this period, learning and growing and happy to be here. They must have been very confused as they tried to reconcile what they knew to be true with what the world was saying about us. That certainly wasn't in the plan.

Graduate Profile:
CHONDRA

In case you hadn't heard, New Philadelphia, Ohio, is the center of the world. Well, at least the center of Chondra's world. It is two hours from Cleveland, two hours from Columbus, and two hours from Pittsburgh. It's her home base as she travels interstate highways to visit friends and work three part-time jobs—one in Akron, one in Pittsburgh, and one in New Philadelphia.

Chondra has always enjoyed adventure. When she was growing up, her family often traveled to camp in neighboring states. She and her brother loved being out-of-doors, exploring mountains, rivers, and caves.

When Chondra was a little girl, the receptionist at her doctor's office intrigued her. Someday she wanted to be the one who got to hand out those fun stickers to kids. Her initial desire to work in a doctor's office has migrated to an interest in nursing. She plans to move to Columbus to attend nursing school next year. Chondra would love to work with kids and is leaning toward working in the field of neonatology.

As she entered New Philadelphia High School, she knew her interest in medicine would require a college degree, so she signed up for the hardest classes she could find. She wanted to be ready for college. By the end of tenth grade, she only needed five credits to graduate and asked the school to allow her to attend half-days for her last two years. She wanted to get a job in the afternoons to help save for college. The school didn't seem to have that flexibility so Chondra began looking for a homeschool curriculum. She was afraid that a college wouldn't understand her qualifications if she didn't have a diploma. When Chondra heard about ECOT, she attended one of our orientation sessions and knew we could meet her needs. She could work and go to school at the same time. At the end, she would have a diploma to show to a college.

Chondra's ECOT guidance counselor helped her choose the remaining classes she needed to graduate in one year. Although she thought her teachers were very nice people, Chondra feels as though she pretty much taught herself. She liked going to other Web sites to research papers and assignments. She had ongoing problems with her ECOT equipment and used some of her own equipment to make do. This was frustrating, but the freedom to get a job and graduate early outweighed the inconvenience of the computer problems.

17

ECOT'S SUCCESSFUL STRATEGIES

"Trying a new thing isn't bad.

It's an experience no one else would have."

Chondra Cline, ECOT Class of '01

I'm happy to report that we actually did some things right from the start. With all the decisions we had to make and all the strategies we had to pick from, we were bound to get some of them right. These decisions didn't get as much airtime as the ones in the previous chapter—and they aren't all that brilliant. But they did serve to keep us going through the struggles and the attacks. Here is my Top 10 List of Successful Strategies:

10. Selection of Our Charter School Sponsor

As we realized that the Ohio Department of Education was not able to provide us with effective oversight and guidance, our relationship with Tom Baker at the Lucas County Educational Service Center grew stronger. We were drawn to his insight, leadership, and forward thinking. He immediately saw the power of our idea to revolutionize public education and helped smooth our path everywhere he could. There would not be an ECOT without Tom and his support of our concept. As he granted our charter, we knew we were partnering with one of the greatest leaders of education reform in the country.

9. Parent Momentum

As soon as students began enrolling, parents picked up the momentum to keep the ball rolling. It became a movement, almost like a cause. You know they were struggling to make sure it would work so that there would be a future opportunity for their kids to go to this school. Many of these parents had no choice. They had kids who had been abandoned by the public school systems. ECOT was their last hope.

ECOT was taking on a persona, more than just a brand identity. It had come to represent pioneers, leaders, let's-do-it, forward-thinking, leading-edge people. The parents who came forward with their children knew they were first. They knew they were taking a risk and yet many of them felt they had nothing to lose.

We did what we could from the beginning to encourage interaction among parents. Online chats and parent-teacher meetings
were scheduled around the state. We produced a newsletter to keep
them informed. We knew that the more they interacted with each
other, the stronger the school would be. Parental/teacher input was
also reassuring to the staff, who needed to be invigorated from time
to time with their confidence in us.

8. Timing

I'm not certain that this idea would have worked if it had been
launched one year earlier. Call it luck or good fortune, the fact that
it hit when it did was just when all the necessary pieces came together and fused at one pop. I don't think the explosion could have
occurred a year sooner. Educational software, computing, telephony—all those issues were resolved.

So many entrepreneurial ideas are just a little ahead of their time
or a little late to market. Our entry into e-education as a statewide
charter school was timed just right. Even with all the struggles and
setbacks, it had to happen when it did. The technological infrastructure that supports us needed to see us come on the scene when we
did. It breathed life into a depressed market for technology while
offering a revolutionary solution to our failing educational system.

7. Motivation to be First

Little did she know, but the state school superintendent actually
did us a favor. By turning down the idea of e-schooling hook, line,
and sinker, she kept our only competitor from entering the market
during our first year. The entrepreneur in me really wanted that head
start and I got it by moving my application to the Lucas County
Educational Service Center and convincing them to allow us to be
their only e-school for the first year. By the time our competitor

learned of his denial from the state, we had exclusivity at the only other channel he could pursue.

As I mentioned earlier, this urge to be the first and only at something passes quickly. I now hope that e-schools begin everywhere. Given the challenges of any pioneer, however, it is helpful to not have to deal with competitors for a brief time. It is also a very motivational message for everyone blazing the trail with you.

We had to constantly reminder ourselves that we were at Kitty Hawk. I would tell my staff "You are on the beach where the first plane will be flown." I must have used that Kitty Hawk speech 50 times a day for six months. It's all we had. When you're out of everything and all you have is words, that's what you use. There will be a day when your grandkids, who are learning through e-education, will be proud of the evidence that grandma or grandpa was at Kitty Hawk. We kept going back to the vision and power of our idea. It was exhausting.

6. Talented, Dedicated, and Passionate People

In the early months, everyone took home very little. I put in my own cash to pay them, $60,000 or $70,000. One time, right before we got paid from the state in July, I was desperately running out of money available to help. If you remember the movie "It's a Wonderful Life," I was almost saying, "No, no, how much do you really need to live on this week? Here's your two hundred, what do you need, here's your phone bill," right down to where we were counting pennies trying to keep everyone afloat.

I'm not suggesting that paying people too little is a good strategy, but I know we wouldn't have been successful if it weren't for the sheer grit and determination of our staff to prove that we weren't wrong. I guess you go from passion to determination. Everyone was determined that no one was going to beat us and yet there were times we worked 24 straight hours on a Sunday night through

Monday morning filling in forms and faxing documents to the school districts. We were not going to let the idea die just because some people did not want to see us live.

What I set out to do was find the best possible people who would commit to the early effort, remain with us, grow with the business, and get the reward later. Anyone who needed a short-term reward or payback did not last. And we did have a significant amount of turnover in the first year from people who couldn't hold out. I don't fault them for needing to go elsewhere. ECOT was a pressure cooker and it took a unique personality and level of commitment not to explode.

Once we had our funding and could begin to operate with some idea of our cash flow, we set salaries at or above the market for those jobs elsewhere. Our teachers are making more than they earned in their former school districts. We are not paying close to what the wealthy districts pay, but that is not the norm. We have much fewer payroll dollars going to administrative positions than other school districts. We try to compensate teachers well because they are shouldering more of the responsibilities with fewer support staff.

5. An Eye on Business

We quickly realized that even a small e-school would require massive amounts of capital against revenue. We needed to develop ways in which to fund the start-up of the business. We also had to keep our eyes on the business as charter schools are designed to be put out of business if they don't perform. The simple fact that we can be put out of business if we don't pay our bills makes us a business. Some people who operate charter schools don't understand that fact.

All the charter schools in Ohio and all the charter schools throughout the country that are successful (or considered the most successful) and still viable, ongoing concerns have been run primarily as businesses delivering education. The schools that have gotten into trouble financially and closed clearly point to a lack of business prowess. And like it or not, pure educators are having trouble coming to grips with business profit as a good thing because they come from environments where profit was never an issue.

It is an issue in charter schools. I spent probably a third of my time on the financials of the business—from the balance sheet to the income statement and cash flow statements. And in accounts payable meetings. If I don't do well there, there won't be a school to run. We are in the business of delivering education. Other charter schools don't always get that. They think that there is some divine educator prowess and that only educators can run schools.

4. Going for Broke with a Statewide School

I came to a decision about the scope of the school several months before we got our charter. As a marketing person, I felt that if we were a small, safe, 30-kid school, we wouldn't get the resources or corporate support to make it happen. I basically threw the dice that we were a statewide K–12, general population, come-one-come-all school. I needed the idea to be big enough that corporate America would say, wow. The numbers would then justify involving a million dollars in software; we could never attract that capital for a school of 30 students. And the truth was that it wouldn't cost a whole lot less to do it for 30 students. Economists talk about the economy of scale. We needed 3,000 students to make it work.

This is the build-it-and-they-will-come, "Field of Dreams" school of business start-ups. We couldn't start small. It would not work, not the way it needed to for the students. This approach brings with it an entrenched arrogance that is perceived by those who don't buy into the concept with a passion. In order for it to work, you have to feel impenetrable. That sense has to be conveyed to the partners that you need to join with you to make it work.

My vision for a statewide school could not waver or those who

I needed to understand it would see my uncertainty. I had no real idea whether it would eventually work, but I knew that if it were to work, it had to be statewide. I never doubted that.

3. Good Media Relations

As much as we had wished that the media would take their marbles and go home in April, by July we needed them. On July 31, we had 158 kids. Of the thousands who had called us, we only had 158 because we had had no way to enroll them. Later we would find out that 100 of those weren't really enrolled either. We now needed to step up the effort. We were about to receive a check based on an estimated enrollment of about 2,000 students by the end of August or September at the latest.

We began an aggressive earned media campaign by sending out news releases and posting a couple of people in every radio and TV station all over the state. We needed to get the word out that we were open and ready to enroll students for a quality education. The first press release resulted in a couple of thousand articles, a couple of hundred interviews, a hundred television interviews, and two dozen radio shows. It got to the point that we had more press in our administrative offices than the state house sees in a day. It was almost like a major news event. It hit *USA Today* as well as some outlying newspapers and national publications. This generated an estimated 40,000 to 50,000 phone calls. We were only able to log 10,000 of them due to our limited phone system.

2. Orientations

At the end of August, we had our first parent orientation. We had reserved locations around the state where parents could come in and pick up packets of information and listen to a short presentation explaining how the school would work. The first orientation in Dayton had a few dozen people signed up to come. Three of our managers went to host it. As soon as they arrived, my cell phone started ringing nonstop. Over 600 people had shown up along with numerous TV stations and four radio stations. It was a madhouse.

The next week we had an orientation in Columbus in a theater that seats a thousand—it was full. I remember walking down the aisle. I knew no one in the room. The presenter said, "I want to stop for a minute. I want you to meet someone. This is Bill Lager. It was his idea. He founded the school. And I want you to meet him." Then there was a standing ovation from total strangers. I asked myself why these people were standing up and cheering? Because they had finally found a school where they could send their kids.

These meetings gave us so much momentum and reassured our vision that we could have a statewide school. They began the momentum that the parents continued as the school opened. They made us know that we had to keep going.

1. Learning Adventures

Our model began with the notion that the efficiency and flexibility of learning online would permit students more opportunities for socialization in their lives. We also knew that the bonds that the students would develop with each other would create an interest in meeting each other. Even though the graduates profiled in this book had pretty full lives and didn't look at ECOT as a means to develop relationships with other students, the younger students did.

We formed a separate organization called Learning Adventures that coordinated field trip opportunities for students of all ages around the state. Students, parents, and teachers can identify areas of interest and attend these opportunities. The hands-on experiences are invaluable to connect our students to the purpose of their lessons online. The friendships that they develop on these trips continue online. Because their families can accompany them, the experiences provide a great opportunity for families to spend time together supporting the student's interests. As well, parents can meet other parents.

The types of adventures that have been and continue to be offered are as varied as the subjects that the students study. We try to offer a fun component while creating a solid learning experience. Teachers can follow up the field trips with chat sessions or assignments based on the topic covered. The student may attend as few or as many as they are comfortable with. This is one of the most dynamic differences between ECOT and any other public school in Ohio. It has proven to be one of our best ideas, building the richest educational experience possible.

Graduate Profile:
RYAN

As a student at Ohio Dominican College majoring in Economics, Ryan knows about consumer preferences. She is the ultimate consumer of educational services. She has made conscious choices regarding her education consumption throughout her high school years.

Ryan was attending Westerville North High School in a large middle-class suburb of Columbus, making good grades and feeling fairly satisfied with her education. She knew where she wanted to go with her career and needed a little more flexibility and choice than a large public high school could offer her.

Ryan chose a homeschool curriculum for eleventh grade because she had more control over which subjects she studied. She also signed up as an intern at the county prosecutor's office, working five hours a day. She did record checks, signed people in to the court, and logged cases into the computer. She liked the six months she spent there and her experience confirmed her interest in the law as a career.

When Ryan heard about ECOT, it was an easy choice to switch from homeschooling. Two things were attractive to her: having teachers again and not having to complete the extensive paperwork required of homeschoolers. More benefits, fewer hassles—two things that most savvy consumers look for.

At an accredited school with certificated teachers and a curriculum she trusted, Ryan found it easy to find the motivation to do her work. She found the curriculum easier than much of her work at Westerville schools and enjoyed her English and writing assignments. She liked having the freedom to explore her writing skills with more independent help from a good teacher.

The delay in getting her computer put pressure on her to finish her work in less time than she would normally have for a year's worth of schoolwork. She was shocked when a teacher actually yelled at her over the phone for not completing an assignment on time after she had experienced down time with her computer equipment. Ryan had never been the type of student to claim that her "dog ate her homework" and she certainly wouldn't have claimed that her "dog ate her computer." She assumed that the teachers would know automatically who wasn't able to get online.

During her year at ECOT, Ryan applied to Rocky Mountain College in Montana where her brother and his family are located. She was excited about getting to know her nieces and nephews better while enjoying the Rocky Mountains. However, she made a choice to stay in Columbus for another year and is attending a small liberal arts college, Ohio Dominican. She plans to transfer to Rocky Mountain for her sophomore year.

Ryan is majoring in Economics and may change to Business Administration. She knows that either will be a good balance to her law degree as she plans to work with corporate law. Her consumer instincts and personal discipline will be assets to any business that is lucky enough to have her choose to work there.

18

PARTNERS IN PIONEERING

"ECOT was a worthwhile education."

Ryan Heilig, ECOT Class of '01

When I was the business manager at our Attorney General's office, I saw firsthand how a government agency buys what they need. I wish I had a nickel for every bureaucrat in the country who wished they could pick up the phone, call someone they trust, order a boatload of whatever they need, and write a check. Purchasing is a tedious, time-consuming, and, ultimately, an unproductive activity for governments. On the surface, the bid process appears to bring the best price for the taxpayers but, in the long run, it does nothing to build relationships, ensure ongoing maintenance, or create good-will. It also virtually requires that governments suspend any inclination to be innovative. How, exactly, do you write bid specifications for something that doesn't exist yet?

Schools are caught in this dilemma. Arguably, schools should be the leaders in thought, curriculum development, and creativity, but how many times do we see curricula at the college level lagging way behind the "real world" applications of those disciplines? Schools are never leaders; they are always followers. Businesses needs to take the risk, invest the capital, make the mistakes, and test the results. Then, as those businesses take their products into the school marketplace, they are required to participate in a bid process. It isn't surprising that the quality of the public schools continues to decline.

On top of the requirement to send large contracts and purchases out for bid, school districts often don't pay their bills on time and the merchants have little recourse to collect. More than one vendor has been put out of business by a bureaucrat who didn't understand the impact cash flow has on the stability of a business. Sometimes, there is even the attitude that if you are requiring payment, there must be something wrong with you.

It doesn't take long before a company doing business with a school district learns the ropes and figures out how to bid contracts. The emphasis is on the here and now, not on the future of the relationship with that district. Even if they do the best job imaginable, a company can still lose the next round of bidding to a newcomer who beats them on price. It's no wonder that vendors are not willing to invest in speculating on new ideas that school districts might buy. They have such low profit margins (if any) on that block of business that they need to cut out all extras.

Our vendors know that we are a privately managed school and, therefore, their attitude is completely different from their attitude toward a government agency. A public school does not usually engage in partnerships for the mutual benefit of the vendor and the school. They look for the cheapest price and the vendor delivers what they pay for. We, in contrast, are running our school like a business and the vendors know it. We know the language they speak and the process becomes a real partnership. When a government agency buys from the marketplace, they don't really understand what's important to business.

They overlook the simple and undeniable fact that the vendor needs to make a profit in order to sell them the products or services they need. That profit is the return on the capital invested that allowed that vendor to exist at all. Profit has even become a dirty word in some circles, believe it or not. It's amazing to me that in the largest free market economy in the world we allow our government employees to hold this attitude. Profit is why that company is there. Profit is why that company continues to be there to offer the products and services that schools need. If a profit margin somehow gets "too high," the market will correct by attracting competitors to that industry. It doesn't need a government bureaucrat to make sure that somebody isn't making too much money.

When an organization operates efficiently and is required to be on the ball all the time, that operation looks at itself internally more often. Introspection is a very important part of its culture. At ECOT, we are constantly looking at our systems: how can we do it better, faster, cheaper? It doesn't mean we cut back. We're in the process of improving our phone system to give live phone answering to all our parents who call in during all hours of the day. We understand that the parents are our customers and should be treated as such. Since we know that we are a business that can go out of business, we must take care of our customers in order to grow.

When you understand the dynamics of profit and your vendors know upfront that you understand, they become your partners. They're there when you need them. They fix things after they've sold them. It's horrendous when Columbus Public Schools buy something and get absolutely no follow-up from vendors. With the relationship public school districts establish with vendors, they do not encourage partnerships. The attitude of the vendors is—you bought it at the cheapest price, you fix it. And it's very hard to get another vendor to come in to fix a problem with the first vendor's equipment.

There have been other factors, as well, that have contributed to our being able to build partnerships with vendors. Having a new idea, a whole different way of delivering products (curriculum, computers, Internet services, etc.), has given vendors the exciting idea that we may be the beginning of a whole new marketplace for them. This has resulted in our getting prices from several partners below what they had bid to larger school systems. From their perspective, they are willing to invest a little upfront in terms of lower profit margins in order to be there to grow with the industry and us.

In fact, we've tried to engineer our contracts to be what I call a back-ended contract instead of a front-end contract. Traditional schools use front-end contracts. Give me your lowest price for this computer, oh, and by the way, what are the warranty and service levels? We do the reverse. What is going to be your service long term if we give you a five-year contract and then what is the price of your computer? What's happened is that we get an excellent price upfront and vendors have a real good assurance of getting the business. We've also included a line in the contracts specifying that if they don't give us the highest level of service, we're going to have an issue. When you do that, your vendor becomes a partner.

We have never seen ourselves as purchasing agents who buy a widget, pay the bill, and wave good-bye to the truck as it pulls away. We are constantly reinventing our systems and we count on our vendors to be at the table with us as we do that. I spend a lot of time building relationships with shared goals with vendors so that they don't have to guess what my expectations are. This takes time but that's part of the key to successful partnerships with suppliers.

A good example of where these partnerships are needed is in the tracking of student progress. Each curriculum vendor we use has their own tracking component, but a teacher has to go into each set of data and then combine them back into one set of records for the student. It would be like getting different long-distance bills vs. getting your long-distance charges on your local phone bill. As we have developed our own Student Electronic Portfolio (SEP) to collect the student's records in one place with standardized reporting, we have needed the support of several vendors. It has been a joint process that will benefit everyone in the long run.

Another factor in building partnerships is the fact that initially I went to people I had worked with over the years, some close to 30 years. They knew me and sensed the power of the idea immediately. As they knew that I would do it with or without them, their initial interest may have been fueled by not wanting to be left behind or to come in second. Very easily, this could be a new industry and, very easily, a lot of new widgets could be sold.

Every vendor is a partner, in our minds, but some of the key partners we engaged to get the school off the ground are important to note. By including them here, I would like to thank them for their initial and ongoing support of quality education for the students we serve. They were climbing the mountain with us as we discovered what would and would not work to build an e-school. Just like us, they had no blueprint, no roadmap, and there were no blazes along the trail.

Xerox Corporation

The initial decision makers at Xerox came from several divisions including educational, electronic, and government. Even within Xerox, a partnership that could each grasp a piece of what needed to be done had to be formed between divisions that would be involved in our project. They already had a division that did this kind of work called the Connect Division, which is engaged in computer programming, telephony, and distance technology.

I had worked for Xerox as a lobbyist after I left the Attorney General's office and before I started Office Works. We went to Xerox, not thinking of them as a copier company but because of their reputation as an innovator and early adopter of ideas. If you go back to who invented the original computer, it was Xerox. Who still holds the patent for the mouse, the icon, and the Ethernet? Xerox. Had we gone to IBM, it probably would not have been adopted. It's just not the culture of IBM to lead. So we went to Xerox because some of the old guys who were there when Xerox was the leading innovator in the world were still there. We were able to use that fact to motivate them to join us. This was the company that registered more patents in the 1970s than any other company in the world. Thirty years later, we wanted them to join us in leading a new industry.

They liked the concept and then there was the question of, "What are our risks?" The risks were high. But they were willing to take them because of their personal relationship with me, because they were innovators, and because they thought this thing could probably work. We were able to encourage them to start down the path. We were so successful, in fact, that before we opened our doors we had spent in excess of $1.8 million with them, all on trade credit. They were at risk.

What does $1.8 million buy you these days at Xerox? They essentially built the infrastructure of our school. If we had been putting up a school building, which can easily cost more, they would have played the role of the general contractor with most of the work being done by their employees. We needed people who could ramp up quickly. We had from February to July to make this happen. We needed a company like Xerox who could put a hundred talented individuals to work immediately and pay them for us, while we waited for our initial payments from the state of Ohio.

Voyager

As the Internet Service Provider with the largest footprint (coverage area) in Ohio, we immediately targeted Voyager as a potential provider of services for our students. As we began negotiations, there didn't seem to be anything that they weren't willing to do for us. Their team of very creative salespeople immediately understood our vision and saw the potential for their company. Even as large as they were, they were not used to getting an order for thousands of installations at a time. However, they were willing to make the necessary adaptations to their equipment statewide that would give us the secure Intranet we required. They had the size and the financial stability to allow us favorable trade credit, which allowed us to grow during those initial critical months.

As we were forced to test their system quickly and difficulties were discovered, they showed a willingness to work through those problems with us. This commitment to the concept and our company could not have been stronger. Their initial pricing was reasonable although not a deep discount over their competitors. As we became their largest regional customer, they reduced their pricing to strengthen our partnership. Even though they knew that it would have been difficult for us to replace them as a supplier and at significant cost, they have always treated us as a valued customer and looked for ways to enhance our security and improve the quality of the service received by the students.

Uvonics

Uvonics is a small computer consulting firm in Columbus that acted in the role of our chief information officer as we built the network. They provided the technical supervision of all the various technology vendors (Xerox, Compaq, Ameritech, Voyager, Learn.com, ChildU) and created the design of the system that would appear seamless to students and teachers.

A principle of the company was a friend of mine for many years and I trusted him to be the glue on the technology side. Given the impossible deadline to pull together something that had never been done before, what Uvonics did was nothing short of a miracle.

As I have detailed throughout the book, the first year was full of technological migraines. Uvonics was the company supervising the solutions to each of the problems as they were discovered. Without them, we would have had six or more vendors looking at each other for solutions. Uvonics was the liaison that kept them all working together.

They continue to be an integral part of our ongoing technology team. As consultants, they are charged with keeping us abreast of the newest technological advances and how they may be beneficial to ECOT. This partnership will keep us on the cutting edge. The fact that they were there from the beginning and lived through all the start-up challenges gives them a unique position to know how to help us grow and gain efficiencies in the future.

SBC/Ameritech

With a protected monopoly at the time we began the school, SBC/Ameritech served just over half of our students. We needed them to provide the students with a local dial tone to connect with the Internet Service Provider. They didn't flinch when we dumped 1,000 installations on them at once.

The challenge was that because they are a regulated monopoly, they could only provide basic services known as tariffs. Our need to do a job fell into the cracks between the products they were authorized to sell. They made numerous attempts to design products that would meet our needs; each time they were shut down by regulators. An example was our request to prevent our students from placing long distance calls. They tried every way they could imagine and ultimately failed.

We also ran into a challenge with their pricing. Even though these were residential lines installed at our students' homes, they charged us commercial rates because we were paying for them. This was explained as a tariff problem as well. It appears that the managers at Ameritech would like to be able to work with us the way our other partners have but are constrained by the government control that affords them their monopoly. We expect that as local competition is expanded, some of these constraints may be relaxed.

The one area where they were able to strengthen our partnership was in their customer service delivery. They have provided us with one contact person for all services so that we do not have to explain to all their staff each time we call who we are and what is happening. This was a much appreciated step forward.

Microsoft

Knowing that Apple Computers had taken an aggressive market position in the education market, we had a big decision to make. We knew that very quickly we would become the leader in K–12 e-schooling and set the example for schools to follow us. The decision was made to create an environment that would prepare students for the computing world they would encounter after they graduated. And that, my friends, is Microsoft Windows.

We knew that we might be eliminating certain education software from our options and causing some confusion among our teachers who had only used Apple computers. We had to weigh this against the acceptance by the parents (who, if computer trained, were likely Windows users) and the state of Ohio, which approved of Microsoft as well.

No other company is doing more to advance technology in education, both as a business and through their nonprofit foundation, than the Bill and Melinda Gates Foundation. They have an opportunity to partner with us to lead the e-schooling revolution. They just don't know it yet. They are a unique kind of silent partner at this point but very soon they will become very vocal as they understand what we are doing—together. Mr. Gates, give me a call, partner, we need to talk.

Compaq

Compaq bent over backward and was helpful and cooperative from day one. Their representative met us during a time when we were interviewing computer suppliers. He did a better job than the others of selling his product and following up with us. Compaq immediately took on the cause of charter schools and embraced the entire vision of e-schooling.

They were willing to build up machines to our specifications. What we needed was not a normal production item. We had to assume that our students would not have any computer skills when they opened the box. The computer had to work quickly with minimal installation. They continued to work with us to make this happen.

They brought in the officers of their financial corporation and scheduled a debtor meeting to discuss the ECOT concept. We knew that we needed to lease the computers and that we would not have cash to pay the lease payments until after they would need to start building the computers. This, again, was capital provided by a vendor through their subsidiary finance company. It was critical to our success.

The technology of PCs is continuing to change and our ongoing relationship with Compaq is helpful in keeping us aware of options as our needs change.

ILC

Another leasing company that provided us start-up capital filled in the gaps when the capital from Xerox and Compaq was not enough. Like everyone else who saw this concept at the moment we were two phone lines sitting on milk crates, they had tremendous ability to envision both the need for the school and the solutions that lay in technology. They partnered with us to make the school happen in a way that they might do for one out of a thousand companies that approaches them for capital. We didn't look like anything they had seen before, but the numbers made sense and the concept had great probability of success. They also saw the strength of the other partners that had already signed on to provide capital. The risk they took was highly calculated. They are savvy financiers and helped me learn a tremendous amount about good financial management.

ChildU

I have stressed throughout this book that I am a businessperson by training, not an educator, but I have to admit that our premier curriculum provider is one of my favorite vendors. ChildU shares my zest for innovation and they never stop thinking and creating new and wonderful methods of learning. They are a true partner in innovation. We learn of their latest ideas first, get trial versions of their newest products, and have the opportunity to give them feedback that makes their designs work perfectly in our school. They have been quick to respond to our needs to have them tighten their security protocols and make other technical adjustments.

Initially, knowing that we were a start-up company with huge potential, they gave us pilot pricing. In a way they also provided us with working capital—curriculum for less than market price—giving us a chance to develop a relationship with them and deciding what would work for us. Everything has worked wonderfully.

The other partnership we have with ChildU is the thought leadership of the e-schooling industry. Several schools have started because of their leadership. They are constantly referring people interested in starting an e-school to us for guidance. Together, we are promoting and helping to build e-schooling into a new industry.

Learn.Com

This company is our cyber classroom that we access through our server. They are the lesson plan book that the teachers use to communicate their assignments. You could also think of this site as the student's "homeroom." This is where the interaction in the school takes place.

We have an ongoing daily working relationship with Learn.Com. They are totally involved in responding to any security issues and other modifications we need to run our school. They assist our teachers in creating their online classrooms. They modified the structure of their products to help us out. We are the first to get to try new features that they design as well.

Our partnership is critical, because unlike many of our other relationships, what they provide us is what students actually see on their computer. They create much of the image that the student has of their school.

We are thrilled with all our partners. They not only saw the vision and took the leap with us, they have stuck with us through the tough start-up period to help us create the wonderful, functioning school that we have today. We do not let them rest, however. We trust them to act in our students' best interest, although we do verify their performance. Our emphasis is on building strong, long-term partnerships with companies that continue to bring our students quality services.

They are not done, by a long shot, in this game of bringing quality education to the children of Ohio. Tomorrow will bring more exciting strategies and solutions. Our relationships with these leaders in their respective fields ensure that we will be among the first to know what those systems are and we will be able to evaluate them for our uses.

Graduate Profile:
JACOB

Jacob sometimes wonders why his coworkers at the engine factory are still making the same mistakes that he made in middle school. He is happy to say that he made just about enough bad judgment calls growing up to last him for a lifetime. He has learned from those mistakes and is focused on a positive and productive life with his new wife and baby son.

Jacob never saw school as a means to an end. Instead, it was a system to be worked. How many classes could he miss before someone would notice? How many tests could he flunk before he'd have to take the class again? Which classes were the easiest ones to sign up for? In a way, I pity his son because that kid is never going to get away with anything— his dad will know exactly what he is up to!

Jacob knows that it took intelligence and effort to get away with the things he pulled in school. And his antics didn't always go unnoticed. When his family moved from St. Louis to Cincinnati after tenth grade, the system there caught him more often. He entered eleventh grade with half the credits he should have had. He finished that year with a very interesting report card. He had flunked almost every course except for two classes in Audio/Visual technology—the first two As he had ever achieved.

Jacob had finally found something that interested him enough to show up for. He did his work; he studied for tests; he helped the teacher with extra projects. Then he went to talk to a counselor about transferring to a two-year vocational educational program in A/V at another Cincinnati school. She looked at his grades and agreed.

By signing up for this program, Jacob was asking to go to school for an extra year. As a kid who had always looked for ways not to go to school, this was out of character. In this program, he would attend the vocational program in the morning and return to his home school in the afternoon for his academic courses. Knowing he would never make it back to class at his home school, he asked for permission to take his other credits at the vocational school. The counselor helped him do this.

This program was a privilege and Jacob needed to meet slightly higher standards to stay enrolled. His old habits were hard to kick and he found himself regularly skipping his afternoon classes. He was aware of the attendance requirements and was carefully calculating his performance. Just as the second year began, he contracted mononucleosis. He missed three weeks of school and passed the threshold for absences. He was ineligible to continue the program.

In November of 2000, he was a fifth-year senior and still needed more credits to graduate. He spent one week back at his old school and knew it wasn't going to work. He visited the counselor again with the plea to help get him out of there. He wanted to graduate but knew he couldn't do it there. She had just heard a rumor about ECOT and said she would check into it for him. The more Jacob learned about it, the more he liked it.

Jacob knew he was out of options. He had worked the system to the point where it had nothing left to offer him. ECOT was his last chance and he knew it. He had never seen himself as not graduating. He had only wanted to do it with the least effort possible but he had miscalculated.

Once he signed up for ECOT, nothing was going to stop him. He did most of his work on paper for the first couple of months. Then he used his own computer for much of his work, while waiting for the computer issues to be resolved by ECOT. To his surprise, he found himself working faster and harder on his assignments than he ever had. He liked setting goals for his work that day and then exceeding them. He worked at home, with no one to push him. It was all up to him. There were no systems to work and no friends to impress.

All those years Jacob was missing class weren't totally wasted. He spent a lot of time on his passion of music. He plays the bass and the drums and continues to enjoy playing in bands. He is still in touch with the A/V teacher who sparked his interest in that field and is currently evaluating his options for returning to school to pursue his dream of combining his two interests. Editing music videos is his ultimate goal.

19

WORKING THE SYSTEM

"ECOT was there for me when I was ready."

Jacob Keach, ECOT Class of '01

We all know what traditional schools look like. Whether public or private, we can envision the principal's office and his or her secretary sitting in the school office. We can hear the bells ring telling the children when to start and stop studying. We can picture the kid on his way to the principal's office for mouthing off in class. We can feel the anxiety of each student as a test is handed out. We know the excitement of the first day of summer. It's a system we understand. We each lived through it 12 or 13 times and then again as our children experienced it.

From the perspective of the professionals that provide educational services, it's a system they understand also. I hear young girls talk about wanting to be teachers so that they can have their summers free with their children when they become mothers. They know that teaching is one of the most challenging, yet rewarding, careers. Teachers live by schedules and rosters and grading periods and test scores. The creativity of teaching is packaged inside a very structured system.

ECOT also has systems, just not the kind you would associate with a school. Our school is "open" 24 hours a day, 7 days a week, year-round. Our students are free to attend school in the middle of the night, during Thanksgiving dinner, or when they are sick. Our teachers are also free to work whenever they choose, understanding that their work loads usually add up to more time than a classroom teacher puts in. They work from their homes, some caring for small children as they work. I can bet that not many diapers were changed during Chemistry class when you were in high school.

Understanding the communication systems in place at ECOT will help you see the most startling differences between e-schooling and traditional schooling. Talking is highly controlled in a classroom. The teacher has the apparent authority to decide when to speak and the students receive permission to speak from the teacher. In e-schooling, there are no such parameters. If a child is reading along in an assignment and has a question, he doesn't need to raise his hand for permission to speak. He types an e-mail message and sends it to the teacher. The teacher may answer it immediately or later that day after she is finished with other duties. The answer is private and specific to that student's needs. The students are inclined to ask more questions because there is no chance of looking stupid. If several students are experiencing the same problem, a teacher can invite them to a chat session to cover the topic again or to share insight with other students. The teacher can also phone the student if a more involved discussion is required.

The ECOT teachers are finding that their students develop a high level of trust with them and that they are the recipients of some very personal and often tragic cries for help. Students have communicated suicide threats and stories of physical and sexual abuse through e-mail and phone conversations. We have needed to establish a system to immediately bring other professionals into that student's life to help with problems outside the scope of educational concerns. Teachers in traditional classrooms also hear these issues, but because no one else is "listening" at ECOT, students may feel more confident to share their problems.

Each day, as the teachers and administrators check their e-mail and voicemail messages, they have learned not to expect any day to be like the previous day. The system is working because they take each problem as it appears and work with the parents and students as best they can. Our teachers have no model to follow and no mentors to consult. In fact, they are now called daily from other e-schools around the country for their insight, as "veterans" in this industry (which is still not old enough to go to Kindergarten). The stress that this puts on the teachers is undoubtedly different from the stress of traditional classrooms. PDAs and day planners are not much help. Flexibility is the key.

Our three principals, our director of education, and our superintendent have similar days. Many of the challenges and questions that roll up to them are beginning to feel standard, while others are still brand-new and must be handled with compassion and creativity. They have given up trying to control their schedules and each works long hours, keeping their cell phones charged around the clock. Over 500 phone calls and thousands of e-mails come into our main office each day. Our elementary school, middle school, and high school are each larger than any other school in Ohio, with over 900 students each. In a traditional school setting, three or four principals might be assigned to this many students.

The principals supervise teachers who are isolated from each other physically and who sometimes need more moral and professional support than other classroom teachers. They are often nervous about the negative publicity surrounding e-schooling and fear for their jobs. In the first two years, it was difficult to recruit teachers to this new and innovative approach to education. The teachers who joined us are pioneers in their own right. As the word has spread, we now receive dozens of applications each week from teachers who would like to be part of this revolutionary change in their industry. This has lessened the pressure on our principals to keep the school fully staffed with top professionals. It also feels good to know that we have gained the respect of so many members of the educational community.

The relationship between the teacher and the student is still the key to an effective educational experience and success for the student. We have heard from several of the kids that ECOT taught that the relationships they developed with their teachers were different from any relationships they had experienced at their previous schools. They loved the increased attention and thrived academically. We also hear that it is possible to procrastinate and ignore their teacher as the teacher isn't standing right over them every day in class forcing them to do their work.

Our system requires two things that traditional schools do not:

1. Direct involvement of parents

2. Personal commitment from the student

We have found that many of our parents are transient and unstable, either financially or emotionally. Some move frequently and don't tell us. Sometimes we have to put on a private investigator's hat to find our students. In these situations, the students are at the mercy of their family's situation. It is true that we can take education to the child, wherever they are. This requires, however, that we know where the child is. I imagine that this same child would be changing schools frequently in any school system. E-schooling cannot automatically fix the inability of parents to focus on the importance of education for their children.

If a child was good at working the system in a traditional school, they will quickly find out that our system is much easier to work. We have attendance requirements that ask the student to log on to our network at specified intervals and they must submit activity logs that ensure they have received instruction and academic activity for the required time periods. The parent is responsible for supervising this reporting, much as the parent is ultimately responsible for making sure that a student goes to a school building each day in a traditional system.

Many students who enrolled at ECOT did not initially understand that ECOT would mean more work, not less. Their image of staying home to go to school was that it would be easy to ignore assignments, watch TV, and play video games. This group of students is our hardest challenge. We are evolving our system constantly to address their needs. It is a challenge that educators have dealt with forever and we need to adapt strategies to fit our environment. Our school is designed for various ECOT families. We try to fit every need that comes our way. This takes a great deal of coordination. In traditional schools, you know where your students will be for the day. Our students are all over the state and online at all hours of the day and night.

Teachers and principals are usually sheltered somewhat from the politics of education. However, at ECOT they find that a lot of time is spent troubleshooting issues that normally do not come up in traditional settings. Far too many of our families have been pressured to return to their traditional schools by their local district superintendent and by the truant officers in their school district of residence. Some of the parents fight for the right to choose where their children attend schools. Others give in. The political issues take a great deal of our teachers' and principals' time. In traditional schools, they did not have to prove their school's right to exist.

One political official who opposed ECOT was visiting our offices. She was sitting in our director of education's office when a mother poked her head in to say hello. It was obvious that the mother had a brain tumor as the tumor had left the confines of her skull. She had driven to the Columbus office to thank the people who allowed her to be with her child as she went to school. The mom is spending the last few months of her life with her daughter without sacrificing her daughter's education. When the mom is too sick to help school her, the child's grandparents pick her up and take her to their home where she is also set up to get her schooling with us. When the mother dies, the custody of her daughter will go to the grandparents. The child will still be in the same school even though it is hours away in a different part of the state. For this politician, seeing this mom and her daughter said more than I ever could.

For all of the staff who deal with reality like this every day, it is clear why they do what they do and why they work so hard. It is equally hard to reconcile why the rest of the world can be so critical of their work. The media seem to focus on the negatives about our school and not on the miracles that can occur on a daily basis. Much of our in-service training has been to try to help our teachers cope personally with the traumatic lives that our students lead. When we tear down the standard boundaries of school, more details of our students' lives creep into our teachers' consciousness. We don't have a bell that rings at 3:00 p.m. that signals the teachers to stop caring and go home.

Schools have dozens of systems that come together to make the educational experience work for the student. From how they take attendance to how they select curriculum to how they hire the teachers, efficient patterns evolve that allow the entire institution to work. At ECOT, every one of those patterns began at the same moment and is still evolving. The computer systems and connectivity, the accounting systems, the human resource systems, the purchasing systems, the teaching systems—all of them are works in process. There has not been one employee who has looked at his or her work and declared, "Well, that's done!" They all know that they are part of the most dynamic and exciting school in the country and that it is their job to keep it changing until every child in Ohio receives the education he or she deserves.

Graduate Profile:
Autumn

School is boring, work is boring, Ohio is boring. Autumn even admits that she is boring. Music, however, is a totally different subject. There isn't an instrument she can't play or won't try to learn. Autumn doesn't know where her talent came from, but it has been there since she can remember and has created a passion that she won't let go.

Living north of Dayton, Autumn was a student at Greenville Junior High and then at Bradford High School. She joined every band and ensemble they had. With only 150 kids in the high school, there were plenty of spots to fill in the various groups. It reached such a pitch that by her sophomore year, she had burned out. Autumn realized that her skill level had moved her beyond the programs the schools offered and she dropped out of them.

With music gone from her school day, there were fewer reasons to get up in the morning. By her senior year, Autumn resented having to spend six hours at school to take the only two classes she needed to graduate. She would leave school and rush to work at a grocery store to put in a full eight-hour shift, getting home at midnight. Waking at seven the next morning to go back to a place she hated was extremely stressful.

Autumn's dad heard about ECOT and knew how unhappy his daughter was with school. The instant he mentioned it to Autumn, she was in.

She remembers feeling as if she had been saved. She certainly didn't want to drop out so close to graduation after 12 years of effort.

Autumn quickly found that there were benefits to ECOT other than not having to physically go to school. She knew she arrived home from work each night at 11 or 12 very alert and eager to do her schoolwork. She found working until around 3:00 a.m. the best time to do her schoolwork. Her brain worked better, the house was quiet, and she could concentrate. Then she would have plenty of time to sleep and get herself ready for work the next day.

With her new enthusiasm over school, Autumn found herself getting to know her teachers and enjoying the weekly chat sessions. She also liked e-mailing the other students. Sometimes she found that she would let certain assignments go and then have to do them at the last minute. She was forced to develop an internal sense of discipline that had previously been supplied by the structure of her classroom teachers.

After graduation, Autumn continued to work full-time and still prefers the second shift. But work is just a job, giving her time to establish her independence and take a break from school. She thinks about college more and more. Maybe in another year, she'll be ready to return to school. She'd love to study music and theatre. She's not ready to predict where that will lead her but, whatever career she chooses, it won't be boring.

20

RAISING THE BAR

"Schools need to be more flexible in order to let
students pursue their own interests."

Autumn Davis, ECOT Class of '01

My goal of keeping the game alive does not imply that it never changes. In fact, just the opposite. The more you play, the better you get. The better you get, the more you want to play. Never rest. Never settle for achievement defined by someone else. Keep raising the bar. The day it feels easy, you've lost.

It certainly has never felt easy at ECOT. But we're still playing and we're getting better. When we first started, the vision was clear, but the possibilities were unknown. As the vision became reality and the possibilities loomed bigger than anyone could have imagined, it was overwhelming for a while. After two school years, our expectations are beginning to be in line with our potential. We are setting realistic goals and carrying out projects with achievable deadlines. For an entrepreneur, this starts to feel boring. For a business, a school, and its customers, however, it begins to feel exciting. It feels as though our future is more predictable. We don't have to guess what might happen—we can plan what will happen.

Our plans for the next school year, which we will be starting as this book is released, are exciting. Some changes are continuing reactions to errors we made during the first two years. Some changes are possible because of new technologies. And others are just good ideas that have come out of two years of experience and a better understanding of our students' needs.

To give you a sense of where we are going and the ever-changing dynamics of e-schooling, I will share with you, in no particular order, initiatives that will be allotted resources during the next school year.

Special Needs Curriculum Modifications

Each of our special needs teachers supervises the curriculum adaptations for 36 students. Each student has six lessons per day. Do the math: Over 200 lessons per day that might all be different! Our goal over the next year is to begin to capture these modifications in curriculum models that not only meet the state standards but also give our teachers more efficient access to effective strategies. This is a huge undertaking, but we know that this is an area where e-schooling is especially valuable and has great potential to make a significant difference in the lives of millions of students across the country.

Marketing Efforts to Partner with Local School Districts

ECOT currently has more students than one-third of the school districts in Ohio. Many of those smaller districts are resource poor and cannot add specialized programs to their curriculum. Advanced Placement courses for high school seniors are one example. A small school district may only have three students interested in AP Physics. They could not afford to hire a teacher and dedicate the classroom space for this course. They could, however, have an ECOT computer in their library that the students share, taking a Physics course with 50 other seniors from around Ohio with an ECOT teacher.

Higher Security Protocols

When I think of all the meetings I have sat through discussing security in cyberspace, it's hard to believe that there is more we can do. In general, security involves more structure to our Intranet and less reliance on the Internet. The more we grow and the more publicity surrounds our existence, the more we entice unsavory characters to try to connect with our students online. Every brick-and-mortar elementary school has occasional reports of "suspicious men" cruising the neighborhood. Alerts go out to parents and children are cautioned. We know that there are pedophiles cruising the Internet who are anxious to turn down our street. It is our job to keep the roadblocks impenetrable.

More Educational Web sites

The other security concern regarding access to the Internet is where the children may end up. There are untold numbers of inappropriate and dangerous sites that children can access without proper controls. Most Internet "babysitters" screen out bad sites. Our system takes the opposite approach—we screen in good sites. This can be frustrating to someone who is used to doing a Google search and getting 47,000 hits. It is a very expensive and time-consuming process to evaluate sites for their acceptability for children. We are planning to subcontract with a company that provides this screening service for multiple school districts, providing a hundred times more sites for our students to use in their research.

Specialized Curriculum Delivered on CDs

Since most of our students are using phone line connections into our server (as opposed to high-speed cable or DSL) we are still restricted somewhat when it comes to graphics downloads. Many of the curriculum developers are very good at what I call "jumping bunnies" that excite the children. We plan to deliver some of this type of curriculum to our students on CDs next year. These CDs cannot be copied and will only run on ECOT computers through some clever programming tricks. This is important because we have to ensure to our suppliers that the products will not be shared with non-ECOT students. We want our suppliers to stay in business and get paid for their excellent products. We do not want to be the source for originals in a black-market curriculum business.

Partnership with Columbus State Community College

Columbus State Community College was one of the first two-year colleges in Ohio to offer distance learning via the Internet to its students. Ohio has a post-secondary option program that allows high school students to take college courses (at participating colleges) when they have exhausted the courses offered at their high schools. As the school district pays the college, there is no cost to the student. We are forming a partnership with CSCC to facilitate this option for ECOT students. We hope to have selected courses available through our Intranet to our students.

Students Who Are Not Self-Motivated

If I had ranked this list, this would be number one. We have a group of students who need to be coerced into doing their work. Primarily in the upper grades, these students do not have active parental supervision and have never taken school seriously. We are installing a series of both positive and negative motivations that we hope will impact the performance of this group. We are also installing outcome measurements that should tell us which of our strategies make a difference. This is one of those uncharted areas where we are totally on our own. We hope to document our research well so that other e-schools will not have to reinvent this wheel.

Working with Dropouts

One of the most underserved populations in our state are young adults between the ages of 16 and 21 who have not finished their high school education. The General Equivalency Diploma is the only option they are given. The culture of public high schools does not welcome them back should they choose to return. ECOT is welcoming them eagerly. They are some of our most motivated students. Having been out in the "real world" for a couple of months or years, they see the value of that diploma and the education that leads to it. Most of them need to work, however, and enjoy the flexibility of online learning. We plan to actively inform these young adults that ECOT is available to them.

Using Only ECOT Computers

During our first two school years, we gave parents the option to allow their children to use the family's computer to "go to school" at the ECOT server. During the next year, we will be eliminating this option for two reasons: (1) We cannot guarantee their security and (2) we will be able to enhance their learning experiences (e.g., CD curriculum) if we control the hardware they are using. Very shortly, we expect the cost of laptop computers to come into the range of affordability so that a student can study in multiple locations.

Phone Line Ownership

We give up. We can't fight human nature. The initial strategy to own the phone lines and pay the bills directly was intended to ensure continuous phone service in the student's home and make sure that no financial burden was placed on the parent. But, without the phone company finding a way to block long distance calls for us, we were eaten alive. The kids couldn't stop themselves and we couldn't collect from the parents. Beginning in our third year, we are changing this system by paying a stipend to each student for their phone service. They will receive a higher stipend if they install DSL or cable modem service. For families with more than one child, our stipend should pay the entire cost of high-speed access. They will be responsible to pay the bill, including any long distance charges.

Improve Standardized Test Results

The state of Ohio currently runs a proficiency test system in fourth, sixth, ninth, and twelfth grade. The system is migrating to the federal system over the next few years. Whatever testing is mandated, an e-school has a more difficult task getting the children to take it. Testing sites and proctors have to be arranged and the children have to show up. We have installed incentives to ensure this performance, such as receiving their phone service stipend. While getting students to the test is an obvious first step, student performance on the test is an underlying goal in all the educational standards we have installed. We are also installing pre- and post-test measurements for each course to measure the effectiveness of the curriculum as well as the student's progress.

In-Service Training for Teachers

The kids that ECOT taught were all instructed by teachers who had never taught online before. They were pioneering ways to transfer their classroom skills to an online classroom every day. Many of them were learning computer skills at the same time. No one has yet defined the entire skill set necessary to master this type of teaching. We are beginning quarterly in-service trainings devoted entirely to the new skills necessary to become an effective online teacher. Our teachers are all learning from each other at present. These in-service sessions will start to document and organize the strategies that they find are working. This information will be available to teachers across the country as new schools form and new teachers switch to this teaching method.

Screen E-Schooling Candidates

As a public school, we will never tell a child that he or she cannot attend our school. We might, however, help parents evaluate whether this method of education is likely to be successful for their child. We hope to conduct research and develop evaluation tools that potential students can easily use. This type of entrance evaluation can also help us identify students who are likely to be successful but who will need some modification in their approach. It might also identify parents who are not likely to be satisfied with the approach.

In-House Repair Depot

When a student's computer needs repair, it is essential that we get it running again quickly. In the next year, we will be doing the repairs to the students' computers in our own facility. We can ship them a loaner and repair their system quickly. We will also use this facility to recycle computers coming back in from students who have graduated or moved.

Electronic Report Cards

The next module planned for the Student Electronic Portfolio (SEP) is an electronic report card. At this time, records are maintained online, although report cards are actually printed and mailed. I know this sounds almost ridiculous. It was just one of those things that kept getting bumped for the crisis of the moment. Next year, it should happen.

Upgrade Enrollment Packets

We have rewritten our enrollment packets to comply with new state regulations and to improve record keeping for new students. This should help parents find all the information they need as their student begins their ECOT experience and help us make sure we have received what we need to keep the state happy. This was one of our biggest challenges in the first year and each year we make huge improvements.

Accrual Accounting

Our financial reports that are filed with the state are required to be on a Cash Accounting Basis. For the nonaccounting-minded person, it means that if we don't pay our bills, we can make it look as if we have a surplus. As a business that we are running like a business, we need to use an accrual accounting system to make sure we match our revenue with our expenses. We now have a system that will create both sets of books for us: one we need to run the business and one the state needs to compare us to other schools.

Next year the list will, no doubt, be different. The future holds possibilities for new approaches to education that have not made it into even casual conversation, let alone formal policy debate. The last three years of my life have been the most energizing and tiring time of my life. Change is never calm, especially when it happens so quickly. The change that ECOT has demonstrated is threatening to many people, although I wonder how anyone could feel threatened by the kids that ECOT taught. All of them have found pride in their choices to be part of this revolution and comfort in their abilities to enter adulthood as productive and positive citizens. We all owe them thanks for reminding us that the energy of youth holds the promise for tomorrow.

Graduate Profile:
JAMES

Since the pilot episode of "ER," James has known exactly what he wants to do with his talents. He found his passion early and has never wavered. His father worked for several years as a firefighter. James saw firsthand the dedication, courage, and stamina that his father exhibited and set that example as his goal. As a Seaman Apprentice attending the United States Naval Hospital Corps School in Chicago, James is well on his way to becoming a trauma doctor.

James joined ECOT for exactly one reason: to facilitate his quest to become a physician. He felt that the self-paced curriculum would allow him to graduate a year early, enter the Navy a year early, and get a head start toward the dozen or so years that it normally takes to complete the degrees and residencies he needed.

From the day that James decided to attend ECOT, he viewed our quest to be the first statewide charter e-school as inspirational. He accepted from the start that there would be glitches and fought right alongside for the concept. He knew that he was helping make history. He describes the computer problems as minor compared to the major impact this innovation will have on public education everywhere.

He was proud to be from Lucas County, where our concept was embraced and chartered. He says he got to meet Tom Baker once and was impressed with the man's vision. He describes the entire effort as similar to jumping into the deep end of a swimming pool without knowing how to swim, and somehow surviving. Nobody knew what was ahead and nobody could have known. Chaos was everywhere, yet a few committed individuals kept their focus and continued fighting. James knew, without a doubt, that we were focused on him and all the other students who would benefit from this revolutionary approach to education. He is forever grateful for our efforts and willing to travel anywhere to testify to the benefits of e-schooling.

James and his family moved a few times while he was growing up. As he wasn't the best at forming new friendships, he stayed mostly to himself. He knows that this personality trait helped him in high school because had he not been so quiet, he might have been targeted as a nerd. His focus on his education was certainly not the way to be popular at his public high school. He knew what he needed to do to reach his goals and he didn't care for a second what his classmates were up to.

In public high school, James saw the workloads that the teachers were carrying and knew that they didn't have the time to work with students individually. At ECOT he was thrilled to actually get to know his teachers and counselors. He had set a rigorous goal for himself—completing one and a half years of credits in one year. He credits one particular ECOT counselor for believing in him and working nonstop with him to help him reach his goal. Even though he knew the ECOT teachers were struggling with the start-up problems along with the students, they always responded whenever he needed help.

James is a proud young man. He is striving to develop his skills to the point where he can be truly helpful to those in trouble. As a member of the Navy, he is proud to be able to serve his country while he works toward his goal of becoming a doctor in an emergency room. He is not deterred by the reality of staring at blood and guts for a living. He sees all of us at ECOT as the education trauma docs, not daunted by the blood and guts being spilled every day by the condition of our public schools.

21

AS THE WALLS
COME DOWN

"Most of the people who criticize e-schooling are just
afraid of change. What I did was participate in the first
step of opening the door. All we have to do is open it
all the way and everyone will get to experience the
benefits of what e-schooling has to offer."

James Gerrity, ECOT Class of '01

All of our lives are structured around boundaries. In the areas of business, government, and education, political, economic, geographic, and cultural boundaries give our world a certain kind of order that allows society to function. ECOT, in a very real way, has started upon an idea that will have an effect of tearing down those boundaries—or at least making them less visible. When we have something that can be delivered at any place at any time, we also have something that can challenge the way we structure things.

We know that we can provide an education to a child in a rural Appalachian community in Ohio that barely had phone service last week. We know that we will provide an education to someone who is confined in a hospital for a year. By being able to do this, we redefine space in our culture. Schooling is no longer confined to a definition of a particular space at a particular time. Learning is available to the child when and where the child is available to learn.

We will also see the weakening of boundaries within government. We tend to compartmentalize and define functions in society as separate from each other. But we've never succeeded at isolating the finite needs of children. Everything about their education is intertwined with every other aspect of their being. Because educators were the first to successfully gather children together on a regular basis, other professionals charged with caring for children began to add their agendas to those of the educators. This diluted the effectiveness of the educators and strained the system to the point of virtual collapse.

The holistic integration of these programs and, therefore, the integration of the needs of the child will only be met as these boundaries come down. E-schooling, by its nature, will begin to provide an integration of learning and the corresponding cultural change in that learning. In the future, a public health threat to children will be dealt with swiftly and effectively by the public health officials through the e-schooling system without diluting the focus of the educators. In our current mindset, we expect teachers to put aside their learning plans for that day and address the more imminent need. Both agendas are important and both can live side-by-side in an e-schooling culture.

In Ohio, Governor Bob Taft recently merged two agencies charged with the well-being of families and workers. The new Department of Jobs and Family Services was formed out of the Department of Human Services (aka Welfare Dept) and the Ohio Bureau of Employment Services (aka Unemployment Office.) And there are so many more agencies serving families and children: Department of Youth Service, Department of Rehabilitation and Corrections, Department of Education, Department of Health. In all those cases we have separate compartmentalized political entities that keep their agendas separate. Computing, itself, has begun to change this. For example, take the efforts being made to catch parents who aren't paying their child support.

The public schools now employ social workers and counselors. The mental heath agencies employ teachers. The health departments employ community educators. The police departments employ drug abuse prevention specialists. The lines are beginning to blur. E-schooling will allow more direct access and individualized services for children everywhere. Imagine the ability of the State Department of Health to facilitate a virtual support group for children with juvenile diabetes. If every child is linked to the network that hosts that support group, just think of how we can break down the boundaries that that disease creates for a child.

One of the best examples of how these boundaries need to come down is to look at the situation of pregnant teenagers. The Department of Jobs and Family Services may provide support and even housing for a young woman, but the Department of Education has great difficulty continuing to provide her with the education she deserves and needs more than ever, now that she has a dependent to support. When something happens to a child that takes him or her out of a traditional environment, the systems tend to shut down because they are isolated and apart from each other.

In our short time with ECOT, we have already found that there is a glimmer of hope that multiple departments can work together for the best interest of the child. By being able to follow the child into the social service setting or juvenile justice setting, we are breaking down the barriers of the education system. A juvenile judge can remove a child for rehabilitation and be comfortable that she is not removing the child from an education. A doctor can order appropriate medical care for a child and the family does not have to choose between the child's health and the child's education.

When all the arguments are in, the single biggest determinant to a child's lifelong health and well-being, socially and economically, is that child's level of education. If a child's access to education is removed, prospects for future success diminish exponentially. Yet, every day, a short-term problem caused by a medical issue, legal issue, or social issue will bar another child from his or her education. I am in no way advocating that we ignore the short-term problems. Nor am I advocating the abandonment of the traditional school structure that has worked for many children for many years. Instead, I would like to share my excitement that there is now an affordable option that enables us to continue educating a child while caring for the child's short-term crisis.

Boundaries will come down slowly—at the top of each agency's agenda is self-preservation. Those who work inside the two agencies that Governor Taft merged are still not happy about losing their identities and probably never will be. Employees who go through corporate mergers show this same attitude. Self-preservation is very natural and needs to be understood. E-schooling has the power to creep into areas where education has never had a presence before. As school boards and education departments find that they no longer have any excuses to disenfranchise any student, they will need to work more closely with the agencies that have, in the past, picked up the pieces when they let a student go. E-schooling will change the way government looks at children and education and health and welfare and corrections and law enforcement.

The expected initial reactions from the established education industry, including the government officials, the school employees, the unions, and others is to fear e-schooling as an attack on a system that they have built. In a big way, it is. But in a bigger way, as soon as they embrace it as their own, they will find themselves with a bigger market, more success in service delivery, and a shifting of the power structure in state governments. They will also find that they will be able to focus more directly on the delivery of education services while enabling other professionals to address the other various needs of children.

The future impact of e-schooling on K–12 education will be explosive. The ECOT model we developed that has shattered the earlier definitions of what an education looks like is just the beginning. I predict that within 15 years, every school district in the country will have their own e-school. There will be dozens of models and creative applications of this technology that has just been uncorked. The genie is out of the bottle and will be granting the wishes of parents and students everywhere. As consumers, they will communicate their choices and the public officials will have no choice but to listen.

My brain doesn't have enough space for all the permutations that these consumers might design in the future, but let me give you some hints as to what they might find interesting.

Computer Labs

Almost all schools have computer labs already. Let's think about how they might change in the future. Right now, there's a room with tables and computers. The student is scheduled or allowed on his or her own time to sit in the room and log onto a computer. They can use various software programs provided and in many cases access Internet resources. They might have a personal folder on the school's network where they can store their work. They would primarily use the computer to (1) learn computer usage skills, (2) complete assignments, and (3) do research. In some labs they might also be exposed to computer programming skills.

In the future, all students could have their own access to their assignments and their progress in a course. They could post questions for their teachers to answer outside of class. They could e-mail teachers and other students. They could turn in homework electronically and take tests on the network. If they change schools, those files could follow the students and they could pick up right where they left off.

Additional curricula could be programmed into the school's network or be available through the Internet. Students who want to study comparative religion, American sign language, Impressionist art, or other courses that a teacher may not be available to teach, could receive credit for completing coursework through the electronic delivery system. Teachers could monitor their progress without needing to schedule specific class time to meet with them.

Remote Access to Computer Lab Tools

A student could call into the school's computer from a computer at home to do their homework, complete research, or communicate with a teacher. All the functions of the computer lab could follow them home for after-hours activities or classwork on days they are ill. During a recent proficiency test preparation period in a nearby school district, students were provided with a password to an Internet site that allowed them to take sample tests. This password also worked from any Internet connection. Students with computers at home could continue their practice after hours. The parent could also have instant and complete access to their child's progress.

Curriculum Delivery Enhanced by Classroom Experiences

Right now the classroom is the primary delivery mechanism, with homework second and e-learning third. What if that order were reversed? Homeroom could be the time spent reading the posting from teachers and planning your day's work. The classroom would then become the hands-on or instructor-led enhancement to the core assignments of reading and research. The teacher would have more time to customize the student's experience and respond, often confidentially, to the student's questions.

Class Schedules Restructured

As hardware technologies reduce in price, each student can be issued a laptop computer that can dock at various places or be connected through satellite networks to the school's server. They might only spend half the time they now spend in the actual school building. They could work from home part of the day or part of the week to complete their assignments and participate in classwork. This would allow older students to have more flexible work schedules and allow all students to do their assignments at a time when they are most capable of learning.

E-Only Classes

To combat the growing teacher shortage, schools could contract with educational software and contract teaching firms to supplement where the need is greatest. Instead of closing students out of popular classes and forcing them to adjust their demand to the school's supply, the school could automatically increase their supply of certificated teachers through an e-course delivered through the school's server.

The integration of traditional schools and e-schools is a natural. Initially the addition of e-schooling options will be a defensive move for a school district: "If we don't offer e-schooling, the students we want to keep will leave and go elsewhere." As they offer e-schooling because they have to, the motivation will shift to a positive motivation. They will see its value and unlimited potential and want to make a better e-school. Right now superintendents are bound to be against the idea of e-schooling because of the funding mechanism. Their initial attitudes have been formed by money, rather than what is in the best interest of the children.

School principals, on the other hand, who aren't as directly concerned with funding issues, see e-schooling as a way to solve their biggest headaches—children who don't fit in at their schools. The change will come from the grassroots—the parents and principals of these students. The irony is that, for a while, these cast-offs of the traditional system will receive a better education than they could have in the old system. Their diplomas will begin to be respected more than the diploma they would have received at their traditional public school. Then the other students will want the same benefits. The district will not want to send them away and will find ways to bring innovative delivery systems into their districts.

A school district can afford an e-school with two students. As soon as the superintendents begin to adopt e-schooling, it will occur in several ways. The large urban schools will establish their own e-schools within their district, at first as a place to put the students that they have expelled. The wealthier small, generally suburban districts will begin to offer e-schools to provide an opportunity to extend the educational experiences of the students they have. They will initially develop their own models and then begin to aggregate resources and contract out more services. The small resource-poor, generally rural districts will contract initially for specialized services like gifted programs.

Other private providers of education will adopt e-schooling models and services, probably faster than the bureaucracy-heavy public system. Private schools with reputations for producing the best SAT scores can break down the barriers of distance when attracting the best students. Wealthy parents can "send" their children to boarding schools without being separated from them for long periods of time. They could adopt similar strategies to some colleges, where residency is two weeks a quarter, with all other coursework delivered through distance learning mechanisms. International educational opportunities would take on very new possibilities when the students can still be connected daily to their home school.

We've all heard, and often joked about, the stories of our great-grandparents walking several miles in the snow, uphill both ways, to get to school. The sacrifice they made was not questioned. Education was the way out of the poverty and circumstances that their physical isolation created for them. As we built more schools and bought more buses, that journey became shorter and easier. Transportation to school became a right, not a privilege, and education became a mandate for all children. These changes did not happen by accident.

Today, we get the children to school rather safely. School bus accidents are rare and buses usually arrive on time. Now we question the appropriateness of the one-size-fits-all approach to public education. Parents have spoken with their dollars and their votes: They want choices in education for their children. They know the cost to the child and society of leaving even one child behind. E-schooling will be the choice that opens the world of quality public education to every child.

The e-schooling revolution that we are living through right now will be seen by history e-books as the biggest change since the beginning of public education itself. Those 21 pioneer graduates of the ECOT Class of '01 were just going to school, the same way that their great-great-grandparents went to school. Uphill, both ways.

GRADUATES OF
THE ECOT CLASS OF 2002

At the time of publishing, the following students are from the ECOT graduating class of 2002. I wanted to extend my congratulations and thanks to each of them and their parents for helping to continue our tradition.

Christopher R. Aey	David Crawford
Katie Alkire	Heather Davis
Sheena Bailey	Sherry Doane
Anthonio Barksdale	Thomas Doering
Sean Baughman	Shawn H.T. Dye
Karla Becker	Brandie Farley
Jonathan Bradley	Silas Gossman
Ronald Breeze	Emmalea M. Green
Amanda Campbell	Christina E. Gute
Heather Carroll	Jack D. Gute
Misty Clark	Thomas Jr. Hall
Lorial Colbert	Darcie L. Henson

Jenifer Irvin

Burton C. Jakupca

Suzannah Johnson

Michael Kane

Blagoyche Karovski

Amanda Kinison

Dusty D. Long

Crystal Malone

Melissa Maljan

Chris Mazerall

Amanda Meadors

Jordan McDonald

Danielle Miller

Dustin Moore

Andrew Nunn

Darryl Ocacio

David Peek

Christopher Pickett

Renee Powers

John Roller

Julie Rosselot

Daniel Ryan

Daniel Sheppard

Hailey Smith

Christy Stapleton

Amy Starkey

Jennifer G. Sutherland

Michael Talbert

Amy L. Tropkoff

Anthony Tully

Lacey Wallace

Amber West

John Williams

Sherrolyn Young

PUBLIC POLICY AND CHARTER SCHOOL RESOURCES

American Association of School Administrators
1801 North Moore Street
Arlington, VA 22209-1813
703-528-0700
www.aasa.org

American Federation of Teachers
555 New Jersey Avenue Northwest
Washington, DC 20001
202-879-4400
www.aft.org

American Legislative Exchange Council (ALEC)
910 17th Street Northwest, Fifth Floor
Washington, DC 20006
202-466-3800
www.alec.org

California Department of Education Charter Schools Office
School Fiscal Services Division
560 J Street, Suite 170
Sacramento, CA 95814
916-322-6029
www.cde.ca.gov/charter

California Network of Educational Charters
744 El Camino Real
San Carlos, CA 94070
650-654-6003
www.canec.org

Center for Education Reform
1001 Connecticut Avenue NW, Suite 204
Washington, DC 20036
800-521-2118
www.edreform.com

Charter Friends National Network
1295 Bandana Blvd., Suite 165
St. Paul, MN 55108
651-644-6115
www.charterfriends.org

Charter Schools Development Center at the California State
University Center for Education Reform
6000 J Street, Foley Hall, Room 327
Sacramento, CA 95819-6018
916-278-6069
www.csus.edu/ier/charter

Colorado Department of Education
Colorado Charter Schools
201 East Colfax Avenue, Room 402
Denver, CO 80203
303-866-6771
www.cde.state.co.us/index_charter

Colorado League of Charter Schools
7700 West Woodard Drive
Lakewood, CO 80227
303-989-5356
www.coloradoleague.org

The Heritage Foundation
214 Massachusetts Avenue, Northeast
Washington, DC 20002-4999
202-546-4400
www.heritage.org

Massachusetts Department of Education
Massachusetts Charter Schools
350 Main Street
Malden, MA 02148-5023
781-338-3000
www.doe.mass.edu/charter

Michigan Association of Public School Academies
215 South Washington Square, Suite 210
Lansing, MI 48933
517-374-9167
www.charterschools.org

Michigan Department of Education
Office of Education Options
608 West Allegan Street, Hannah Building
Lansing, MI 48933
517-373-3324
www.mde.state.mi.us

Michigan School Board Leaders Association
P.O. Box 608
Davison, MI 48423
810-658-7667
www.msbla.org

National Association of Elementary School Principals
1615 Duke Street
Alexandria, VA 22314
800-386-2377
www.naesp.org

National Association of Secondary School Principals
1904 Association Drive
Reston, VA 20191-1537
703-860-0200
www.nassp.org

National Association of State Boards of Education
277 South Washington Street, Suite 100
Alexandria, VA 22314
703-684-4000
www.nasbe.org

National Charter School Clearinghouse
7532 West Indian School Road, Suite B
Phoenix, AZ 85033
623-846-2530
www.ncsc.info

National Conference of State Legislators
444 North Capitol Street N.W., Suite 515
Washington, DC 20001
202-624-5400
www.ncsl.org

National Education Association
1201 16th Street Northwest
Washington, DC 20036
202-833-4000
www.nea.org

National Governors Association
444 North Capitol Street
Washington, DC 20001-1512
202-624-5300
www.nga.org

National Middle School Association
4151 Executive Parkway, Suite 300
Westerville, OH 43081
800-528-6672
www.nmsa.org

National Parent Teacher Association
330 North Wabash Avenue, Suite 2100
Chicago, IL 60611
800-307-4782
www.pta.org

Ohio Department of Education Community Schools
25 South Front Street
Columbus, OH 43215-4183
877-644-6338
www.ode.state.oh.us

Pioneer Institute for Public Policy Research
85 Devonshire Street
Boston, MA 02109
617-723-2277
www.pioneerinstitute.org

Thomas B. Fordham Foundation
1627 K Street NW, Suite 600
Washington, DC 20006
202-223-5452
www.edexcellence.net

U.S. Department of Education
400 Maryland Avenue, Southwest
Washington, DC 20202-0498
800-872-5327
www.ed.gov
www.uscharterschools.org

INDEX

O

Ohio
  agencies for well-being of
    families/workers, 283
  Department of Education, 46, 99,
    178, 221–222
  post-secondary option program
    in, 270–271
  school district, 98–99
  Supreme Court order in, 24
O'Neill, Tip, 131
operating costs, 116. *See also* costs
opposition, sources of, 129
options for school districts, 23
orientations, for parents, 233–234

P

parents
  absentee (physically/emotionally),
    89
  banning of, from education
    system, 162
  benefits of ECOT model for,
    168–169
  as consumers, 60
  as customers, 163
  involvement of, in ECOT model,
    167–169, 261
  with limited abilities, 203
  momentum of, 228–229
  online groups for, 88
  orientations for, 233–234
  support mechanisms for, 86–87
Parent Teacher Associations (PTAs),
  127–128
partnerships. *See also* vendors
  among government agencies,
    283–284

  with Columbus State Community
    College, 270–271
  with local school districts, 269
  public/private, 49
peer criticism/control, 76–77
Perkins, Jennifer, 197–200
phone service. *See* telephone service
pilot programs, for expelled
  students, 89–90
policies, 140, 293–298
political issues
  sheltering teachers/students from,
    262
  state policy decisions, 131
  suppliers of business of education,
    128
portability of ECOT, 261
post-secondary option program,
  270–271
Pounds, Shannon, 65–67
prayer in schools, 70–71
pregnant teenagers, 283–284
principals, duties of, 259–260, 288
print textbooks, 125
private schools, 61–62, 288–289
problems
  of country-wide funding, 98
  with e-mail, 212
  minimization of, for exceptional
    students, 205
  of public schools, 21
  with servers (Internet/Intranet),
    212
  start-up, 217–224
proficiency test system, Ohio's, 272
public policies, resources on,
  293–298